EMOTIONAL CAPITALISTS
The New Leaders

*Essential Strategies for Building
Your Emotional Intelligence
and Leadership Success*

MARTYN NEWMAN

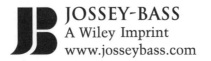

JOSSEY-BASS
A Wiley Imprint
www.josseybass.com

This edition published in the UK in 2008 by   John Wiley & Sons Ltd,

The Atrium, Southern Gate, Chichester,

West Sussex PO19 8SQ, England

Telephone   (+44) 1243 779777

Email (for orders and customer service enquiries): cs-books@wiley.co.uk

Visit our Home Page on www.wiley.com

Under the Jossey-Bass imprint, Jossey-Bass, 989 Market Street, San Fransisco CA 94103-1741, USA
www.jossey-bass.com

First Published in 2007 by John Wiley & Sons Australia Ltd and reprinted in March 2008.

Other Wiley Editorial Offices

John Wiley & Sons Inc., 111 River Street, Hoboken, NJ 07030, USA

Jossey-Bass, 989 Market Street, San Francisco, CA 94103-1741, USA

Wiley-VCH Verlag GmbH, Boschstr. 12, D-69469 Weinheim, Germany

John Wiley & Sons Australia Ltd, 42 McDougall Street, Milton, Queensland 4064, Australia

John Wiley & Sons (Asia) Pte Ltd, 2 Clementi Loop #02-01, Jin Xing Distripark, Singapore 129809

John Wiley & Sons Canada Ltd, 6045 Freemont Blvd, Mississauga, Ontario, Canada L5R 4J3

Wiley also publishes its books in a variety of electronic formats. Some content that appears in print may
not be available in electronic books.

British Library Cataloguing in Publication Data

A catalogue record for this book is available from the British Library

ISBN 978-0-470-69421-3 (PB)

This edition typeset by Laserwords Private Ltd, Chennai, India.

Printed and bound in Great Britain by T.J. International Ltd, Padstow, Cornwall.

To Stacey, Dylan and Scott—
three remarkably intelligent young leaders

Contents

Foreword

In this new millennium, executives either manage people well, or fail.

Technical skills — the bricks and mortar of the past century — are no longer sufficient, and the light is fading on the days when 'command and control' leadership was anything more than a temporary freeze.

As a journalist, I am regularly told that the best new recruits are the ones doing their own interviewing. They are not settling for just any old corporate offering — they want a business to believe in, with real leadership. And it turns out that the mark of leaders who can sustainably manage their teams — and themselves — is their emotional intelligence.

Intuitive executives know this much: that a real ability to listen, to empathise, and to be assertive without being aggressive is vital. They know the bar has been raised: skilled leaders read situations with clarity, and act with independence, decisiveness, and grace. But where does one learn such skills?

Until now, the ability some people have to deal with life and its challenges with apparent ease seemed to be one of those insoluble mysteries. You either had it or you missed out. There appeared to be no rule book. The people who 'made it' in business weren't consistently the best looking, the most outgoing, or had the highest IQ, although having none of these attributes seemed to hurt. The factors that gave a winner 'star quality' appeared intangible, and not reducible to skills amenable to being acquired and practiced.

Rigorous analysis has lifted that veil. And now, it seems, everyone can be in on the game.

Martyn Newman is a consulting psychologist whose work with individuals and across companies has led him to some startling observations about human behaviour, and about how people can change. In this book, Newman challenges the notion that success is limited by birthright, and offers contemporary business leaders a toolbox for personal investment in a new type of capital — their emotions.

More than a catch-cry, what this book also offers is rigour.

Many commentators grabbed the concept of emotional intelligence from Daniel Goleman in the 1990s and ran with it. Few realised Goleman's work had a substantial underpinning in the pioneering work of Israeli psychologist Reuven Bar-On. It was Bar-On's work in the 1970s on emotional intelligence that Goleman popularised. Daniel Goleman convinced us that emotional skills were vital: Martyn Newman tells us clearly how to build them. He has written an accessible text for developing the reader's own skills. His narrative accounts are built not only on his own international experience, but stand on both Goleman's and Bar-On's substantial foundation of evidence from hundreds of thousands of assessments across careers, countries, and continents.

And Newman's good news is that you can unlearn bad habits and take on a whole new set of skills and behaviours that will boost your success: at work and beyond.

Bill Pheasant
Senior journalist
The Australian Financial Review
Melbourne, Australia

About the author

Martyn Newman PhD, DPsych, is a consulting psychologist with an international reputation as an expert in emotional intelligence and leadership.

As well as holding senior positions at leading universities in Europe and Australia, he has had many years of experience working in leadership development and management consulting across Europe and Asia. Martyn has assisted many leading companies to improve the performance of their people and organisation.

He is coauthor of the *Emotional Capital Inventory* and author of the *Emotional Intelligence Sports Inventory* (EQSi) — the world's first EQ assessment of elite sports performance.

He received his PhD from the University of Sydney and holds an MA from the University of California, Berkeley; a Master of Psychology from Monash University, Melbourne; and a Doctor of Psychology from La Trobe University, Melbourne. Martyn is a captivating keynote speaker on the power of building emotional intelligence in the workplace. He spends much of his time between Melbourne and London.

Acknowledgements

This book represents a decade of work on the ideas and practices that have culminated in the theory of emotional capital and new leadership. I have written this book largely in response to the constant prompting over the last decade by my clients, who have asked me to write down the key ideas they have found so powerful in their personal and professional leadership roles.

I am indebted to many who have contributed to my thinking, research and practice. Thank you to Philip Greenway, my friend and mentor, who unwittingly provided the first inspiration for the book. Philip's understanding of the nature of what it means to be a human being and how relationships work best in the real world is nothing short of astonishing. A number of the strategies described in this book have at least their origins in long conversations with Philip. I would also like to acknowledge the work of Kevin Thomson who coined the term 'emotional capital' and provided a valuable account of why it should be included on the balance sheet of every organisation.

Special thanks to Suzy Turkovic for her patience, support, enthusiasm and faith in the value of the work.

Among my colleagues, I would like to thank the RocheMartin team, John and Maria Broderick, for their constant support; and Karola Belton for her willingness to help tell a number of the stories in the book that bring the theory to life. Very special thanks to Judy Purse, one of the finest psychologists I know. Judy's exceptional skills, built on a platform of personal integrity and authentic presence, represent the richest source of emotional wealth in our business. Thank you.

Sincere thanks to Wendy Skilbeck for smoothing out the rough edges.

Thanks to Michael Hebden at Hebden Designs, and the crew at White Rhino, Jeremy, Andrew and Karen Tibbs, for their genius in graphic design.

Thanks to Bill Pheasant from the *Australian Financial Review* for writing the foreword and for guiding me through the completion of the book.

I would particularly like to acknowledge the work of both Daniel Goleman and Reuven Bar-On pioneers in the field of emotional intelligence. They were among the first to chart the course in this exciting territory, and research using their respective models provided the basis for the development of the emotional capital model of emotional intelligence and leadership. The Emotional Capital Inventory provides a robust model of emotional intelligence as well as a valuable tool for measuring the competencies essential to being successful as a leader.

Finally, I'd like to thank the many men and women with whom I've worked over the last two decades. Their stories and our conversations convinced me that emotional intelligence truly can be developed.

No doubt emotional intelligence is more rare than book smarts, but my experience says it is actually more important in the making of a leader.

Jack Welch

Research shows convincingly that EQ is more important than IQ in almost every role and many times more important in leadership roles. This finding is accentuated as we move from the control philosophy of the industrial age to an empowering release philosophy of the knowledge worker age.

Stephen Covey

1 Introduction

What makes you mad, sad or glad? The chances are they are the same things that make your customers and colleagues mad, sad, or glad. We are all the same. Emotions are heartfelt, personal and grounded in your senses. They shape your behaviour, your relationships, your most important decisions and even your economy. That's right, there is money in emotion. In an economy shaped by emotion, success comes from attracting the emotional consumer or colleague — not the rational one. Emotions determine whether or not people will work well for you, buy from you, employ you and enter into business with you. As Jack Welch puts it, 'A leader's intelligence has to have a strong emotional component'.

Elliot was a thirty-something corporate leader with superior intelligence and a bear-trap mind. He possessed a strong grasp of the economics of the business environment in which he operated and had a flawless memory for detail. He was a devoted husband and father, and a role model for his extended family. He wielded considerable influence as a leader in his community and just about everyone who knew him held him in the highest regard and envied his personal and professional success.

Some time in his thirties, Elliot started experiencing annoying headaches, which he initially attributed to a reaction to stress. As they worsened, it soon became hard for him to concentrate. A medical examination revealed the distressing news: a tumour about the size of a small orange was growing fast in the part of his brain just above the roof of the eye sockets — in the frontal lobes. Although this particular tumour was benign, if it wasn't removed it would continue growing and would prove fatal. The good news was that an excellent medical team was able to remove the tumour. The operation was a complete success and, despite this scare, Elliot's future looked very bright.

In the years immediately following his surgery, Elliot astonished everyone as his life began to fall apart. Once known for his independent views and self-reliance, Elliot found it progressively more difficult to make decisions and he became increasingly dependent on others to make choices for him. Although his superior intellect was still evident, he seemed unable to form critical judgements and commit to a course of constructive action. Elliot appeared to lack any ability to manage his emotions or even understand what it was he was feeling at any given time. In fact, most of the time it was as if he had no feelings at all. He was unable to describe what he wanted to achieve and appeared completely devoid of ambition.

His relationships also suffered. Instead of his usual affable personal style, he came across as cold and aloof, and even people who knew him well found him unpredictable and difficult to approach. His personal and professional relationships quickly deteriorated. His wife and family left him and he drifted in and out of relationships. On the one hand, Elliot had no obvious intellectual impairment; on the other, he became inept at work, lost his job, and was unable to keep another. He wasted money in a series of bad financial decisions and found himself living permanently on welfare. Elliot appeared emotionally exhausted — as if he were running on empty.

As the quality of his life deteriorated, Elliot sought the help of a number of medical professionals in an effort to understand why he seemed incapable of taking control of his life. Finally, he saw Dr Antonio Damasio, a neurologist at the University of Iowa.[1] All standard neurological tests came back as normal. In fact, Elliot's performance on IQ tests confirmed that he possessed superior intelligence, a powerful memory and an ability to concentrate intensely and think clearly. As Elliot had jumped through all these hoops so successfully, it appeared that the consistently poor choices that had led to such disastrous circumstances must be the result of a failure in his personality. So, in an effort both to understand his personality pattern and to determine what kind of psychotherapy may help him, Damasio suggested Elliot complete an extensive personality inventory.

You guessed it — once again there was a normal score! A comprehensive psychological evaluation suggested that Elliot's behaviour was not the result of any identifiable personality disorder.

Elliot emerged from this extensive evaluation as a person with a superior intellect and a reasonably normal personality structure, but who appeared incapable of making constructive decisions that affected his personal and social behaviour. At first glance, there was nothing out of the ordinary about Elliot's emotions. But for some reason, he found himself with little motivational energy to start each day, obsessing over minute details and unable to make decisions. Most distressing of all was that he appeared unaware that he had developed a pattern of treating people with a cool indifference that left them feeling confused and often offended by their encounters with him.

I feel, therefore I am

Damasio had seen it all before and quickly established the cause of Elliot's problem. To put it bluntly, Elliot's tumour, which had been successfully removed earlier, had actually damaged tissue in the front part of the brain that supports emotional intelligence. Even though he had recovered successfully from his operation, the surgery took with it his ability to access and understand his emotions. Somehow his intellect remained intact, but he had no feelings about his thoughts, and so no preferences. In other words, Elliot was able to tell you what he thought in any given situation, but could not tell you what he felt, nor understand what other people might be feeling.

This discovery goes to the heart of what emotional intelligence is all about. The physical pathway for emotional intelligence starts at the base of the brain. Your primary senses enter here and must travel to the front of the brain before you can think rationally about your experience. But first they must travel through the limbic system, the place where emotions are experienced.[2] Emotional intelligence requires effective communication between the rational and emotional centres of the brain. The damage caused to the front part of Elliot's brain had taken away his ability to reflect on his emotions. This left him unable to use this information to arrive at accurate judgements and to take positive, constructive action. In other words, he was rich in intellect but poverty stricken in his emotional life.

The rational and emotional centres communicate constantly, helping us to form judgements and make choices. A broadband connection between these centres is critical for developing high emotional intelligence.

In Elliot's case, the connection had broken down, with no emotional resources to draw on to guide hi: Without access to his emotions, he was cut off from of emotional energy necessary to build, drive and motivation. He had no access to a wealth of emotional ex that had been instrumental in his forming sound judge...ents, making clear decisions, solving complex problems and building the sort of prosperous relationships that had characterised his earlier life. Elliot had lost a lifetime of accumulated emotional capital.

Elliot's story is more than just an interesting medical case study. It shows us something vitally important about the platform that supports our personal and professional success. The ability to recognise and respond thoughtfully and creatively to your emotional experience is the most critical factor determining your success. Your best and worst experiences are associated with your emotions.

As you read this book you will discover a blueprint for developing and using your greatest leadership asset — your emotional intelligence — to achieve extraordinary things with ordinary people. This book will provide you with the language to name your emotional experiences and the vocabulary to explain them. More importantly, it will provide you with a practical, step-by-step structure for building effective strategies that will enable you to achieve remarkable results through your leadership.

ACHIEVE EXTRAORDINARY THINGS WITH ORDINARY PEOPLE

Emotional Capitalists — The New Leaders represents a new and very powerful approach to contemporary leadership.

It is founded on three simple ideas. The first is that effective leadership in the workplace is the by-product of emotions such as *self-confidence*, *optimism*, *self-reliance* and *enthusiasm*. The second is that these emotions are valuable because they create strong relationships between organisations and their customers and employees, which, at the end of the day, creates a real competitive advantage for any business. The third is that these emotions and their associated behaviours can be developed and used intelligently to solve problems, create products, deliver superior service and dramatically boost personal and professional performance.

Who are emotional capitalists?

Emotional capitalists are those extraordinary leaders who recognise that to build a successful business today they must go beyond a focus on traditional financial assets, such as physical capital (the bricks and mortar, if you like), and even beyond intellectual capital (which comprises intellectual property, databases, formulas and business processes) to a new focus on emotional capital — the energy, enthusiasm and commitment in the hearts of everyone connected with the business.

According to Kevin Thomson, emotional capital in your business is made up of two core elements: external emotional capital and internal emotional capital.[3] Here I would add a third element critical to the role of leadership: intra-personal emotional capital.

The first element, external emotional capital, is the value of the feelings and perceptions held by the customer and the external stakeholder towards your business. As I've suggested, the only way to create real profit is to attract the emotional rather than the rational customer by appealing to his or her feelings and imagination. Customers want to buy from organisations they like and who are like them. This creates brand value and goodwill and results in repeat sales through customer loyalty, lifetime relationships and referrals. In other words, the brand is more than a name or a logo; it creates trust and recognition and is a promise and an emotional contract with each customer.

The second core element, internal emotional capital, is the value of the emotional commitments held in the hearts of the people within your business. It can be described as the feelings, beliefs and values held by everyone working in the business. As a leader, you know that external customer relationships are important. But your interactions with internal customers — your people — are just as vital. Every relationship that your business has with everyone it touches is an asset and an investment. To build emotional wealth you must treat your people as investors because that is

YOUR PRIMARY ROLE AS A LEADER IS TO CREATE EMOTIONAL WEALTH FOR COMPETITIVE ADVANTAGE

what they are — intellectual and emotional investors. Every day they bring their heads and hearts to work. And if they don't, you won't be in business very long. Internally, emotional capital is seen in the value of the energy and enthusiasm that people bring to work to create products and solve problems.

The third element that makes up emotional capital — intra-personal emotional capital — is the level of positive, focused energy that you invest at work and in your personal life. As a leader, you will inspire or demoralise others first by how effectively you manage your own emotional energy and, second, by how well you mobilise, focus and renew the collective energy of the people you lead.

Frankly, your primary role as a leader is to create emotional wealth for competitive advantage. Nothing in business is more rewarding or exciting. Believe me, I know — after working as a corporate psychologist for more than fifteen years I've seen it many times. Once you put the tools of emotional intelligence into the hands of the people, you open the doors to the remarkable, creative entrepreneurial energy that exists in all genuine leaders.

What are you currently doing that makes everyone who comes into contact with you and your business feel like they're important? You see, everybody in an organisation must be living the dream for the organisation to be great.

EVERYBODY IN AN ORGANISATION MUST BE LIVING THE DREAM FOR THE ORGANISATION TO BE GREAT

And greatness is only attained when leadership creates emotional capital by inspiring everyone to explore and express their own creative contribution to the vision of the business.

To be blunt, the leaders I'm talking about are called upon to build an emotional enterprise — not just a rational one. They do this by creating external emotional capital — appealing to the emotional customer — so that people buy into the brand and organisation. They also create internal emotional capital by treating employees as intellectual and emotional investors in the company. Finally, they pay attention to building and managing their reserves of emotional energy by which they continually renew and inspire others to focus on what really matters.

In the last ten years, the most sensational strategy for achieving these goals has been to focus on developing emotional intelligence. Emotional intelligence is an indispensable set of social and emotional competencies for leveraging knowledge and emotions to drive positive change and business success.

Emotional intelligence — strategy for building emotional capital

There are several approaches to describing emotional intelligence. The term was initially developed by psychologists

John Mayer, of the University of New Hampshire, and Peter Salovey, of Yale University. However, Israeli psychologist Reuven Bar-On had worked independently on a concept he called 'emotional quotient' and first coined the term 'EQ' in the early 1980s. The idea was popularised in 1995 by American journalist Daniel Goleman who wrote the first best-selling book on the subject. Essentially, Goleman summarised the research showing that the 'good guys' — emotionally intelligent men and women — finish first by almost every standard used to measure business success. Simply put, emotional intelligence (EQ) describes a new way of being smart that is more important for success than IQ or technical expertise. It involves two parts: first, becoming aware of how emotions in ourselves and others drive behaviours; and, second, developing the skills to manage these emotions intelligently to leverage our personal strengths to create products, solve problems and effectively influence the performance of others.

Most mature models of emotional intelligence identify four or five broad components. In addition to identifying these general areas, most models break these areas down into a variety of competencies.[4] The emotional capital model of emotional intelligence is a well-researched model that was developed with a specific focus on identifying those competencies that characterise effective leaders. It consists of five broad components and ten specific emotional intelligence competencies.

1 *Self-awareness:* your capacity to understand your own emotions and stay in touch with your feelings. It includes self-awareness, the ability to recognise how your feelings and emotions impact upon your personal opinions, attitudes and judgments; and assertiveness, the ability to communicate your feelings, thoughts and beliefs openly in a straightforward way. This cluster of competencies enables

you to develop your leadership presence and communicate authentically and openly.

2 *Self-management:* your ability to manage your own emotions and have confidence in your ability to manage your personal performance. It includes *self-control,* the capacity to control your emotions well and restrain your actions until you have time to think rationally; *self-confidence,* the ability to accept and respect yourself and essentially like the person you are; and *self-reliance,* the power to be independent in planning and making important decisions and the ability to take responsibility for yourself.

3 *Social awareness:* your talent for tuning into the experience of others. This area includes *empathy,* the capacity to be aware of, understand and appreciate the feelings and thoughts of others. Of course, to be able to understand how other people feel, it helps if you are able to recognise and understand your own emotional experience first. These skills enable you to grasp the emotional dimensions of a business situation and enhance your capacty to influence others to achieve productive outcomes.

4 *Social skills:* your people skills define your talent for interacting and getting along with others. The primary ability in this area involves *relationship skills,* the knack for establishing and maintaining mutually satisfying relationships characterised by positive expectations. This competency, along with empathy, is essential for building the value of the relationship assets in the business.

5 *Adaptability:* your ability to respond to challenges and adapt to new and difficult situations. It involves *flexibility,* your ability to react well to change and adjust your emotions, thoughts and behaviour to changing situations

and conditions; *self-actualisation,* which is the source of your emotional energy and enables you to maintain an enthusiatic commitment to long-term goals; and *optimism,* your capacity to look on the brighter side of life and sense opportunities even in the face of adversity. Optmism determines your level of resiliance and your ability to be able to focus on the possibilities of what can be achieved. Collectively, this cluster of skills enable you to take on new challenges and respond creatively and efficiently to new opportunities.

Emotional capital model of emotional intelligence

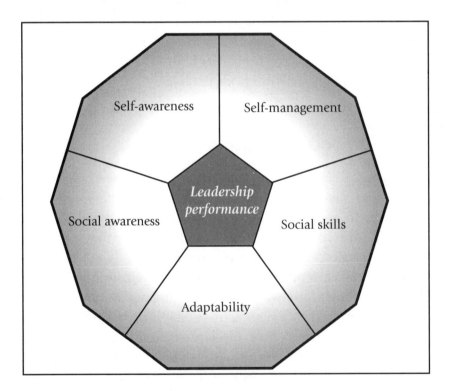

Taken together, these ten competencies are the most practical collection of key success factors that you will find anywhere.

They are important because they encapsulate nearly everything you do that's not a result of how smart you are. Of course, not everyone will have all these competencies in equal measure. While it is true that each of us has a certain 'style' of behaving that defines our personality, how effective you are at handling yourself and your relationships will be captured by a distinctive combination of these EQ competencies. And, as you'll discover, research using the *Emotional Capital Inventory* (ECi) — the world's first psychometric tool specifically designed to measure EQ and leadership skills — continues to confirm that these ten EQ competencies represent the signature strengths of successful leaders. In my experience exploring these ten competencies, there are at least seven that are an absolute priority to focus on. Accordingly, in this book I've chosen to explore what I consider to be the seven most important competencies. The good news is that the research also confirms that high EQ individuals can be made, even if they were not born that way.

'We can rebuild him'

I met John C at a very exciting time in his career. He was a 34-year-old state manager of a global confectionery company preparing to step up to the larger role of regional general manager. John had moved from a marketing role that had been product focused, into a general management (GM) position with ten direct reports and financial responsibility for the region. Although John would be the youngest GM on the team, he was recognised as a high achiever. He had been chosen for this promotion because of his cross-cultural experience and excellent performance record within the company throughout his career. Despite being aware of his outstanding record, both his supervisor, Mark, and the human resources manager, Susan, were keen to appreciate more about the distinctive emotional and social competencies that underpinned his performance.

During the background briefing, Mark, John's supervisor, had remarked that despite John being a good communicator, he was puzzled by the fact that his team seemed passive and less than enthusiastic about his leadership. Susan was also only too well aware of John's relatively young age and was concerned as to whether John had the emotional resources to cope with the demands of this expanded role.

During my discussion with John, he described his signature strengths as having determination and being passionate about what he believed in; possessing good technical, financial and marketing skills; and having sound social skills and a solid work–life balance. I asked him if he had any doubts or questions about his current performance that I could try to help him understand. John didn't hesitate. 'Yes', he said. 'Why can't I get my management team to take ownership of projects?' He also commented that everyone on his team seemed so 'uptight'and scared to take any risks. He then asked, 'Why don't my team open up to me and tell me what they're thinking?' John demonstrated

RESEARCH HAS IDENTIFIED SEVEN EQ COMPETENCIES THAT REPRESENT THE SIGNATURE STRENGTHS OF SUCCESSFUL LEADERS

an obvious enthusiasm for the new role but a little later in the discussion he appeared to be frustrated with himself and commented, 'I see so many opportunities, sometimes I tend to rush at things and get enthusiastic, then things just don't seem to work out the way I expected'. Then, out of the blue, John confided that he had noticed that some people had actually found him arrogant and egocentric. He wondered if I could help him understand more about how he came across, so that he could avoid creating such a negative impression.

I suggested to John that he complete an assessment of his emotional intelligence in order to obtain a snapshot of his emotional and social skills. This would enable us to gather some objective data to try to answer his questions about his leadership style. He agreed and completed his EQ assessment with the enthusiasm that characterised most of what he chose to do.

A review of his profile revealed his highest scores were on EQ competencies such as optimism, assertiveness, self-reliance, flexibility and self-control. These scores went a long way to explaining why John made such an engaging and pleasant initial impact. Scores like this indicated that he possessed a secure and mature personality with a good level of self-esteem and a strong optimistic view of the future. Leaders with these sorts of scores are often characterised by their ability to look beyond the day to day and identify and open up new opportunities. They are usually most effective in 'start-up' and 'turn-around' situations — which was certainly true of John. In addition, John's high score on self-control and optimism suggested that he possessed an enhanced ability to withstand adverse events and stressful situations and would generally cope effectively with the pressure of his new role.

John received his two lowest scores in relationship skills and empathy. Although he possessed strong leadership potential, he didn't appear to be particularly good at understanding and relating to the needs of others.

As we explored his profile together, I suggested to him that maybe because he presented as such a competent, cool and tough-minded individual, with a focus on pushing through obstacles and challenges, he may inhibit openness and team comfort at times. John was curious. I continued by suggesting to him that he was likely to often be misunderstood due to his drive and determination. This may lead him to act quickly and without always communicating sufficiently detailed information to his colleagues. He smiled and agreed instantly, commenting that his wife had often described him as a 'bull in a china shop'.

As we talked further it became clear that John's straightforward but also critical communications style was likely to lead others to back off and avoid taking risks. In his enthusiasm to drive people forward to meet targets he often became so focused on achieving the goal that he did not sufficiently listen to, or take full account of, others' viewpoints or feelings. I suggested to him that if he wanted to get the best out of his people and convince them to buy into his initiatives, then he needed to allow more time for unhurried interactions with them, improve his listening skills and establish a more flexible communications style. Furthermore, he needed to balance his sharp, critical comments with appreciative observations and ensure that he recognised and rewarded his people.

As our conversation deepened, John also became aware that he often struggled with understanding and expressing his feelings. I put it to him that this may suggest that, at times, he will come across to others as 'hard to read' and closed, and that this may go some way to explaining why his team lacked enthusiasm for his leadership.

John appeared to relish the challenge of improving his people skills and enthusiastically took to the program I built for him. I couldn't help but recall the seventies TV show Six Million Dollar Man — you know, 'We can rebuild him …' Although John was functioning extremely well in many aspects of his leadership, his people-management skills needed rebuilding from the ground up.

I met with John again recently and I'm pleased to report that his relationship skills have improved dramatically and he and his team have been taking the region by storm — together!

Can you improve your EQ?

John's experience is further evidence that EQ can be developed. In fact, research supports the view that EQ actually improves with age. The data makes it clear that the older you get the more emotionally intelligent you become, at least up until your late forties or early fifties. This finding is dramatic considering that cognitive intelligence (IQ) has been found to peak in the late teens, level out until the late fifties, and even mildly declines later in life. So, the real question is not so much about whether EQ can be improved — we know it can — but rather, how can we take the necessary steps to accelerate the development of our EQ and leverage these skills to increase leadership success?

ANYONE WHO IS GENUINELY MOTIVATED CAN DEVELOP HIS OR HER EMOTIONAL INTELLIGENCE AND BOOST EMOTIONAL CAPITAL

Although some aspects of emotional intelligence are innate, anyone who is genuinely motivated can develop his or her emotional intelligence and boost emotional capital. I was recently approached by one of Australia's leading international companies, Foster's, to work with the finance team in the brewing division's Carlton & United Breweries (CUB). CUB had identified various behavioural imperatives as drivers of business improvement and was committed to developing these in its leadership team. I took an emotional and social audit to benchmark these behaviours against EQ competencies. I then implemented a development strategy aimed at building the EQ competencies of these high-potential leaders.

Using a combination of a highly individualised EQ leadership and coaching report — the *Emotional Capital Report* — dynamic online modules that broke down EQ into simple building blocks, face-to-face coaching and leadership seminars that modelled EQ behaviours, I was able to demonstrate a 30 per cent increase in EQ competencies over the course of the program. The effect on leadership performance was dramatic, tangible, and, as witnessed through recent follow-up work, highly sustainable.

Emotional intelligence and leadership

Leadership has been described in many different ways. According to Steven Stein, a psychologist and CEO of Multi-Health Systems, 'While there are hundreds of books with formulas for how to be a great leader, there are few studies of what really differentiates the great leaders from everyone else'. Traditionally, leadership has been linked to vision, problem solving, intelligence, technical knowledge and skill. Now, however, there is a great deal of interest in the role that emotional intelligence plays in leadership.

As we have already seen, the Emotional Capital Inventory can be used to identify high-potential employees and, along with the *Emotional Capital Report*, can be used to create highly individualised development programs. Also, a number of recent studies using the Emotional Capital Inventory have identified the distinguishing characteristics of some outstanding corporate and community leaders.

The studies involved several specialist groups of professional people who were regarded as leaders in their fields. Groups included members of Leadership Victoria—an elite group of business and community leaders in Australia; a group from the financial services industry identified as 'high potentials'; and a group of HR professionals from the pharmaceutical industry with specialist roles in recruitment and selection. When scores from these three leadership groups are examined, all scores are significantly higher than the mean on all ECi scales. These studies confirm that there are ten dynamic emotions that set these high performers apart from the average.[5] Although all ten skills are important, as I mentioned earlier, in my experience at least seven of these competencies have a more critical impact on leadership effectivness. Accordingly, these are the particular competencies explored in detail in the chapters of this book.

So, what does it take to be an emotional capitalist and a successful leader?

Emotional capitalists — seven dynamic assets

Interestingly, the research reports of these leaders revealed that they scored high on self-reliance, assertiveness and optimism. In other words, high-performing leaders: take responsibility for themselves; possess an independence of mind, thought and values; are self-directed; are able to express their thoughts, feelings and beliefs in a non-aggressive way; are opportunity sensing; possess the ability to maintain a positive approach; and remain persistent even in the face of major challenges.

In terms of your business, these three competencies enable you to: model self-assured behaviour; communicate a clear view of the organisation's vision and direction; inspire the confidence of others; and deal with setbacks in a positive, constructive way.

These leaders also scored high on self-actualisation. Interestingly, earlier research that looked at predictors of success in the workplace across hundreds of occupations found the one factor of emotional intelligence that consistently showed up — almost regardless of job type — was self-actualisation.

According to psychologist Steven Stein, there are two components to self-actualisation as a skill. The first involves having a passion for what you do — that you love your work and eagerly look forward to starting each day. The second component involves being well rounded. People who score high in self-actualisation have a variety of interests, hobbies and social activities. They ensure that they spend enough quality time in these pursuits. In the process of self-actualising you build emotional capital by producing your best work. Your example, in turn, enables others to believe they can produce their best, too.

Another score that differentiated these high-performing leaders from the rest was their score on self-confidence. Effective leaders have a high degree of self-confidence. Self-confidence is built on the twin emotions of self-liking and self-competence and determines the quality of your relationships. The more you like and respect yourself, the more you will like and respect others, and the better they will feel towards you. Your personal level of self-confidence will be the critical factor determining whether people will have sufficient confidence to enter into business relationships with you.

The sixth dynamic emotion that set these leaders apart in each of the studies was relationship skills. High-performing leaders are better at building relationships. This can have big pay-offs both in developing your external business contacts and in working with your employees. Once leaders start 'telling' people what to do they have already ceased to be effective. Command and control is no longer

LEADERS HIGH IN EMPATHY UNDERSTAND THE TASK THEIR PEOPLE MUST PERFORM AND SENSE THE FEELINGS, NEEDS AND PERSPECTIVES OF OTHERS

in style. If your employees don't buy into your ideas and plans, there is little incentive for them to perform optimally. Successful leaders today focus on winning the hearts and minds of people around them.

When talking about executive EQ at business meetings, one of the questions I'm frequently asked — especially in the presence of female CEOs — is the difference between male and female leaders. Although no overall difference in EQ has been found between genders, female leaders typically score higher than males in relationship skills. In other words, in general, women are better at initiating, developing and maintaining relationships. Relationships represent a unique strategic asset and are the primary source of emotional capital in a business. Managing them well is critical for building real competitive advantage in your business.

One other area that frequently differentiates men from women is the seventh emotional competency — empathy. Although women generally tend to score higher than men, in these studies the high-performing leaders of both genders all scored higher than the average.

The ability to empathise with others is one of the most important competencies differentiating the star performers from the average. Leaders high in empathy understand the tasks their people must perform and sense the feelings, needs and perspectives of others. Empathy allows a leader to create and maintain happy, productive relationships by focusing on the whole person — not just the tasks he or she must perform.

Empathy also creates reserves of emotional capital that can be drawn on when the pressure is on.

The result of this research is convincing and suggests that these seven emotional competencies are the signature strengths of highly effective leaders. Of course, when I speak of leaders I am not referring just to a single individual. Leadership is distributed. In a certain sense, everyone is a leader because everyone is always trying to convince people to buy into what they are doing. Genuine emotional capitalists do not practise leadership; they live leadership. They are what they do.

Time and talent

According to Jonas Ridderstråle and Kjell Nordström, the authors of *Funky Business*, this is an age of time and talent — we are selling time and talent, exploiting time and talent, organising time and talent and packaging time and talent. As a result, emotionally intelligent leadership, with its focus on people and skills, is the key to competitive advantage. How you attract, retain and motivate your people; how you treat your customers and suppliers; and how well your company is led, are the vital differentiators in business today. Today, figuratively speaking, the 'boss' is dead—or at least passé—long live the emotional capitalist!

Workplaces now demand that leaders change by taking on these advanced people-management skills and building their emotional capital. This sort of change does not occur overnight, but it does happen—and 20 years of research confirms that it happens more quickly when seven critical components are present in the learning and development process.

Emotional capitalist — leadership system

Over the last few years I've set about building a rigorous EQ leadership system based on these seven components of emotional intelligence—the same system that Foster's and many other companies have successfully adopted to systematically build emotional capital in their organisations. A description of the 'Emotional capitalist—leadership system' is contained in the appendix, or you can visit the RocheMartin website at <www.rochemartin.com>. There you will find a description of the system and a number of helpful resources for building your emotional capital, including an opportunity to download a sample of the emortional capital report used to help John C make the changes critical to his success. The report provides scores on the ten EQ competencies found to be critical components of effective leadership benchmarked against a large international group of professional people. It also describes a blueprint for individual development together with specific coaching strategies for building emotionally intelligent leadership.

As a reader of *Emotional Capitalists — The New Leaders* you may like to test-drive the Emotional Capital Inventory (ECi) for yourself. The 'Emotional Capital Inventory' measures your personal level of emotional capital quickly and accurately and delivers a summary report of your scores on the seven leadership competencies covered in this book, plus three additional competencies that also characterise effective leaders. To obtain your free promotional code email <contact@rochemartin. com>. The inventory can be accessed online at <www. emotionalcapitalists.com>. Go to 'Discover your emotional capital', select 'Find Out More', enter the promotional code, register your details and complete the inventory. Your report is generated by comparing your responses to thousands of professional people who took the test during the scientific development of the inventory. You may like to purchase the *Emotional Capital Report*, which provides you with an individualised description of your strengths and development opportunities, along with proven coaching strategies to build your leadership success. Visit <www.emotionalcapitalists.com> and purchase your personal *Emotional Capital Report.*

Breaking the EQ code

Sure, emotional capital is a business and leadership philosophy, but as you can see, it's so much more than just a theory. It is a systematic strategy for building wealth in your business.

If the critical components of competitive advantage are things such as innovation, specialised knowledge, exceptional quality, productivity, and attracting and retaining top talent, then they must be something that everyone who comes into contact with your business is committed to. This doesn't occur by adopting a rational rules-and-rewards — or 'sticks and carrots'— approach. And it certainly doesn't happen by using a 'command-and-control' or 'corporate-megaphone' approach. It is achieved by the skillful development and application of your emotional intelligence.

Given that emotional intelligence is made up of flexible skills that can be learned, all that remains is to understand clearly the building blocks that comprise each of these core leadership skills and consistently practise the techniques that build these competencies. Nothing in my business life has been more rewarding than experiencing firsthand what happens when individuals acquire these competencies.

Once you open the doors to emotional capital, it releases an energy within you that will transform both your leadership and your business. In fact, as a result of these experiences I've come to the conclusion that being an emotional capitalist is a way of life — not just a business philosophy. In other words, if you adopt it you will also notice a dramatic improvement in the quality of your personal life.

While there are a number of books that discuss emotional intelligence, and why it is important, this book actually tells you how to get it. The following chapters clearly identify the seven core emotional building blocks that define superior leadership. It then sets out a practical approach for quickly mastering and applying these crucial skills to dramatically increase the emotional capital in your business.

In other words, the remainder of this book breaks the EQ code and provides you with an easy-to-understand blueprint for mastering the seven dynamic emotional assets that will dramatically increase your emotional capital and boost your performance and leadership success.

Welcome to the world of the emotional capitalist.

People are always blaming their circumstances for what they are. I don't believe in circumstances. The people who get on in this world are the people who get up and look for the circumstances they want, and if they can't find them, make them.

George Bernard Shaw

You must be the change you wish to see in the world.

Mahatma Gandhi

2 Self-reliance

What is the single most important signature strength for creating emotional wealth? From the studies of high-performing leaders described in the introduction, the first and most interesting feature in the profile of these entrepreneurs was their high score on the emotional competency of self-reliance. This is perhaps not surprising—after all, how could you run an organisation without independence of mind, thought and values?

Self-reliance is at the heart of the emotional capitalist and this involves two emotional competencies: self-reliance—the recognition that you are a complete and self-directed individual and have the power and responsibility to take decisions and make choices; and self-belief—the ability to have confidence in your judgement and the willingness to take action and put yourself on the line to achieve your objectives.

After all is said and done, self-reliance is a critical emotional skill for leadership because it enables you to act as an essential resource to your people. It is your job to generate the basic attitude of the group and give direction to the decisions that your people are going to make.

But hang on! Before you pick up your corporate megaphone, there's more.

Being self-reliant does not mean that you just go out and do your own thing. It means being secure enough in yourself to turn to others and take into account different points of view while also regarding yourself as finally responsible for working out what has to be said or done. To do that you have to feel competent and creative in situations in which you find yourself. To be blunt, you don't look to someone else for ideas or ways of making decisions, but instead trust in your own creative initiative.

When you boil it down, self-reliance involves having confidence in your own judgement as a leader, and being able to control where you devote your most productive emotional and intellectual energy. This enables you to become a transformational leader who models self-assured behaviour, communicates a clear view of the organisation's vision and direction, and inspires the confidence of others. What an exciting idea!

SELF-RELIANCE INVOLVES HAVING CONFIDENCE IN YOUR OWN JUDGEMENT AS A LEADER

Nothing in my life has been more rewarding than the experience of inspiring colleagues, family and friends to imagine who they are capable of being and what they are able to achieve.

Regardless of any technical competencies you may possess, if you want to lead, you have to look and feel the part. As John Peters,

CEO of Technology Inc., says, 'You can't lead a cavalry charge if you think you look funny on a horse'. Emotional independence expressed as self-reliance and self-belief is essential in becoming an emotional capitalist and building emotional capital in your personal life and business.

Before we explore these two components of self-reliance, here are a few words about how to best think about your role as a leader with a commitment to building emotional capital.

Creativity — the declaration of independence

The most basic difficulty in becoming self-reliant is overcoming dependency and the accompanying feelings of insecurity. Our insecurities are often rooted in the fear of failure or the fear of other people's judgements.

Take, for example, Jason, a logistics manager for a large supermarket chain. When I first met Jason he impressed me as someone exceptionally skilled at the technical aspects of his job. Under his leadership, his division consistently surpassed its quarterly targets. In fact, Jason was considered a regional expert within the supply chain industry. As we talked, however, he confided that one aspect of his role encumbered him with a very difficult challenge. He experienced a real reluctance to manage staff who were performing poorly. Jason acknowledged that he went to considerable lengths to avoid potential conflict. He tended to tolerate underperformance and sloppy work rather than address the issues with the relevant people.

Jason feared that managing people's performance would make him unpopular and imagined the confrontation and disharmony that it would cause. In striving to be a well-liked manager, Jason's lack of belief in his ability to appropriately critique and support his people, and the emotional discomfort this led to, continually undermined the strength of his leadership. His fear of being judged negatively by his staff meant he worked longer hours to compensate for their underperformance. While he was tuned in to the feelings of others and was a good listener, he also found himself reluctant to communicate his views in a straightforward manner. By making decisions guided by how others might react (that is, by what they might think of him), Jason had stopped tuning in to his own thoughts and backing his own judgement. He had actually heard from colleagues that some of his people had described him as a 'pushover'.

People who experience low levels of emotional self-reliance display a range of behaviours that can best be described as 'impression management'. It's as if their lives are structured by the question, 'What will others think?'

Over time, Jason learnt to shift his focus from pleasing others and worrying about their potential judgements of him, to trusting his own views and communicating them clearly. As issues came up, the first question he asked himself before consulting with others was, 'What do I believe?' He would then make decisions based on an inner conviction and communicate these in an honest, respectful and straightforward way (skills we cover in detail in the chapter on assertiveness). Learning to accept responsibility for his own views and behaviour also enabled him to allow others to do the same.

After several weeks of coaching, he told me he felt much calmer and more genuine in his life generally, and more inspired and powerful in his leadership role. This last comment is not surprising. In addition to strengthening your leadership presence, building emotional self-reliance also frees up a lot of creative energy. As your self-confidence builds, you will find yourself trusting your more innovative ideas and taking risks. This is the unexpected pay-off of becoming more independent.

Not only do independent people experience more power, but they also experience more creative energy.

I can hear you say, 'Creativity? You've got to be kidding, right?'

Actually, I'm not. Any way you look at it, human beings are fundamentally creative. Yet in order to express your innate creativity you have to see yourself as a creative person and trust your own creative genius. Opening the doors to your own creative emotional energy is absolutely integral to becoming an extraordinary leader. Leaders high in stocks of emotional capital have little interest in proving themselves, but a continuous interest in expressing themselves.

This is not as easy as it sounds — particularly if you're someone who has spent most of your life working out what others want you to say, do or be.

To lead well, you have to make a declaration of independence against being judged by the estimation of other people. Or, as the German philosopher Hegel put it, 'To be independent of public opinion is the first formal condition of achieving anything great'. In other words, to make a decision to lead is to decide to stop being a product of your time and place and instead take responsibility for creating a distinctive vision and accomplishing something unique. This is what ultimately defines you as a leader.

Strategy one — self-reliance

Leadership is for grown-ups

So, now the journey to finding and expressing the emotional capital within you begins. The most basic challenge of increasing your emotional self-reliance and becoming an effective leader is the same one that you face in becoming a mature adult. As children, we naturally develop a psychology of approval where we seek to protect ourselves against the vulnerability of our helplessness. This need for approval is an effective strategy for having our needs met as children. The problem is that many people carry this psychology into their adult lives. This approval-seeking mindset creates feelings of dependency and powerlessness.

And that's the good news!

At worst, this need for approval fuels a narcissism and resentment that consumes our most powerful strengths, abilities and creative energies.

In practical terms, think of your life as a book — the early chapters you coauthor with your parents, teachers and other influential figures. The choice to become an adult is about choosing to be responsible for authoring your own personal story. To become fully independent you need to overcome the approval-seeking mindset that fuels your insecurities and self-doubt, and accept personal responsibility for who you are, what you become and what you want. This represents the enormous step from childhood to maturity. Prior to that decision, many people go through life wounded, tending to criticise, complain and hold others responsible for their problems. They exhibit what I call the 'Snow White syndrome'.

Some day my prince will come!

You know the story. Life is tough. Through no fault of your own you've been given a poison apple so you think you'll just lie there on the cold slab and wait for rescue. If you're lucky, some time in your thirties you realise the bad news — no-one is coming to your rescue! You've got a decision to make, and it's the most important decision of your life — wake up and get up off the slab! After making that decision, you can begin to see yourself as the primary creative force in every area of your personal and professional life.

To become an emotional capitalist—to create wealth in the fullest sense of the word—you must make the decision to accept personal responsibility and become self-reliant. Self-responsibility is the core quality of the fully mature, fully functioning individual. In fact, in your business there is a direct relationship between how much responsibility you are willing to accept for results, and your value as a leader.

Successful leaders have a strong sense of internal accountability that extends to their work and to all of their relationships. Self-reliant individuals tend to be positive, optimistic, self-confident, and, as we shall see shortly, possess a core self-belief.

I don't need to tell you that the complete acceptance of personal responsibility is not easy. We are conditioned to believe that other people (such as our parents, teachers and colleagues) are to blame for what happens to us. This certainly feels true at the emotional level. After all, it was Freud who originally suggested that 'we are not masters in our own house',

SUCCESSFUL LEADERS HAVE A STRONG SENSE OF INTERNAL ACCOUNTABILITY THAT EXTENDS TO THEIR WORK AND TO ALL OF THEIR RELATIONSHIPS

by which he meant that we are controlled by our primitive emotions. Fortunately, one of his students—and one of my favorite psychologists, Alfred Adler—recognised the creative genius in all of us when he said, 'Individuals can create their own unique lifestyle and are therefore responsible for their own personality and behaviour. They are creative actors rather than passive reactors'. Absolutely!

At the emotional level, perhaps no-one has expressed this truth more straightforwardly than Eleanor Roosevelt when she said, 'no-one can make you feel inferior without your consent'. I'm convinced that Eleanor and Alfred were dead right. Sure, we can all find reasons to blame others for our circumstances and even for our personalities, but in reality you never actually give away responsibility. The only thing you really give away is control. If you try to make someone or something else responsible, you end up giving him or her, or it, control over your emotions. In other words, you are still completely responsible, but by giving up control you lose your ability to direct your life and lead effectively.

At the risk of labouring the point, management consultant Brian Tracey puts it this way: 'There is a direct relationship between how much responsibility you accept in any area of your life and how much control you feel in that area'.[6] There is, in turn, a direct relationship between how much control you feel in any given area and how much independence you express in that area. Responsibility, control and a sense of independence, or autonomy, go hand in hand.

Tracey also suggests that there is a direct relationship between responsibility, control and independence, and the number of positive emotions you enjoy. When you put it all together, the message is simple: there is a powerful connection between the level of overall responsibility you accept and the level of personal emotional capital you are capable of building.

It's time to bite the bullet!

Leadership is what big people do

Self-reliance actually arises from a deep trust that you have the strength to face your leadership responsibilities head-on and overcome the patterns of dependency that have controlled your performance in the past.

You begin to develop your emotional capital as you recognise that you are a completely self-directed individual and have the power to take responsibility to act accordingly. While from the standpoint of your awareness your status as an adult is obvious, you may not be fully convinced at an emotional level.

Pause for a moment and become aware of how often you experience the emotional desire to remain dependent and escape from responsibility. Sometimes this shows up in the paralysis of indecision or through procrastination. Sometimes you may find yourself acting impulsively. Both are typically techniques to avoid responsible, thoughtful choice. In the first instance, you put off making the decision because of the responsibility of living with the consequences. In the second instance, you act quickly to avoid the anxiety of considering all the potential options and outcomes. We all struggle with these options continually.

It was Plato who recommended that 'Whenever you meet another human being remember they are fighting a battle'. This battle inside each of us is often the battle between the two parts of ourselves — the child and the adult. The child in you remains controlled by fear and insecurity and wants to remain dependent on other adults. The adult part of you wants to assert mastery over the fears that sabotage independent, creative thought and action.

Remember, at each moment you are fighting that battle and choosing whether to allow the child or the adult in you to determine your thoughts and actions. Notice that I did not say feelings. To build your emotional capital, pay attention to your feelings and accept them, but examine them in the light of your adult self. Then choose actions that are consistent with someone who is fully independent and free.

It's lonely at the top

Becoming self-reliant is important because, in my experience, there's a certain loneliness that accompanies the leader's role.

There appears to be many situations where there is often no-one else to turn to but yourself. At these times you have to have trust in yourself.

Most of us prefer to talk about leadership as a subject rather than refer to ourselves as leaders. Few people are comfortable with the title of 'leader'. As Michael Gerber says, 'Leadership is what big people do'. Gerber goes on to suggest that to become a leader, you first have to learn to live with the word and accept its importance and responsibility.

WHAT DOES IT FEEL LIKE TO BE YOU?

You have to learn to feel at home with saying, 'I am a leader. I am called upon to do the work of leadership'.[7]

In other words, the first responsibility to yourself as a leader is to become comfortable with the fact that you are a leader. You won't take your responsibility seriously if you can't take yourself seriously. Seeing yourself as a leader is the first task for building your independence — even if you do look silly on that horse!

Of course, this is easier said than done. Let's break it down even further.

The dance of leadership

Think of responsibility as being made up of two components: 'response' and 'ability'. The first part of 'response-ability', response, is the capacity to respond rather than react. When you react to something, you are not making a conscious choice, but instead acting out of habit. The situation stimulates a reaction deep in the emotional part of your brain, which in turn sets you up for a set of learned reactions. The stronger the emotional reaction, the more rigid and predictable your behaviour becomes (and often less appropriate!). Your ability — the second part of the equation — is really your talent. Whether or not your talent shines is determined by the impact of your emotions on your behaviour.

The first thing to understand is that, in reality, leadership is not actually a battle after all — it only feels like one. It's actually more like a dance, because it involves getting your responses and your abilities to work together. In other words, it's emotional capital that makes your talent dance!

You can only be angry about your feelings of powerlessness and dependency if you believe it shouldn't have been that way. Much of your lack of independent behaviour is likely to be a struggle to win approval and acceptance. No matter how hard you try, though, you will never achieve enough or be good enough to satisfy this longing. The best response is to recognise that dependency was perfectly appropriate as a child and no-one is to blame for it — not you, nor anyone else. But now that you are an adult you no longer need the approval or acceptance of others. Instead, you must see yourself as a free, independent person. Once you do this, you can accept yourself in your role as a leader. This deep acceptance of yourself and your role as a leader enables you to develop your leadership abilities.

Showmanship — the lead story

While your leadership should not be driven by the pressure to win approval nor avoided because of the fear of disapproval, you should not minimise the need to demonstrate the abilities of leadership. Zen writer and philosopher Alan Watts wrote about the importance of showmanship as a requirement for success in a highly commercial society. As he put it, 'No-one can succeed as an independent author or minister (leader), without a flair for drama and coming on strongly as a personality, and by success I mean not only financial reward, but also effective communication'.[8] In other words, in order to excel you've got to live in the tension between, on the one hand, genuinely accepting yourself and

WHAT DOES IT FEEL LIKE TO BE YOU AS A LEADER?

being comfortable with who you are, and, on the other hand, continually reinventing yourself as an author of growth and change in yourself and your business.

The message is simple but profound. Leadership is about acting responsibly and telling a story authored by you.

DO YOU TRUST YOURSELF ENOUGH? At this point, let me say what absolutely needs to be said. Deciding to take this step is crucial to becoming an authentic leader. It is the only platform upon which you can build compelling leadership.

Once you have taken response-ability for authoring your own story, one of your primary abilities as a leader is to communicate the story of your business to your people. You must do this with a flair for drama and visibly take responsibility for the vision you communicate.

Being clear about where you are going and why you are going there is your most important response-ability as leader. Lack of clarity about outcomes and about what the end game looks like creates uncertainty in your people. By contrast, a clear and compelling vision provides them with the confidence they need.

Think of it this way.

CSO — chief storytelling officer

True leaders are really CSOs — chief storytelling officers — and the stories they tell become the stuff of dreams. This is where real emotional capital originates. It's the energy generated by the story of what you and your business are capable of achieving. It's this energy that provides the focus, inspiration and meaning that ordinary people as well as organisations need to move forward. Your job is to tell and retell the story of what your business is capable of achieving: where it's come from, where it currently is and where it's going. Most importantly, it's about enabling your people to understand the value of their contribution to the story.

As a leader there are three types of stories that you have to tell. The first is your personal story. To be credible, you have to express yourself genuinely and communicate your beliefs and values in ways that distinctly represent who you are. This is not about wearing your heart on your sleeve, but about describing what makes you tick and what values drive you as a person. For example, if you value diversity and innovation then ensure you create an environment where people's views are respected and taken seriously and where mistakes can be made without retribution. Likewise, if you value collaboration and teamwork, then ensure you're a team player by consulting widely among your people.

WHAT IS YOUR STORY?

The second story you have to tell is the group or collective story. This provides some sense of collective identity with which the group can identify. Leadership is not about imposing your individual dream, it's about developing a shared sense of destiny. It's about enabling each person to develop a sense of belonging to the group. You do this by helping each individual to understand both his or her unique contribution and the distinctive contribution of others. In other words, adopt a 'you need me and I need you' approach.

Once the first two stories are communicated clearly, the real power of your leadership will exist — as it always has — in telling the third story: the destiny or dream story. In this story you provide a description of why the group must change, where it is going and how it will get there.

The destiny or dream story provides people with dreams that touch, excite and arouse them — something that ultimately gives them a chance to live out part of their hopes and aspirations. This story must be genuine and come from your heart. It must be an authentic expression of your confidence in what can be achieved and why it matters. In addition to 'big picture' descriptions, it needs to be reinforced continuously by celebrating small wins, recognising small achievements and commemorating milestones.

DOES YOUR STORY EMPOWER YOU AND ENABLE YOU TO TAKE RESPONSIBLE ACTION?

Harvard leadership guru, Howard Gardner, also believes that leaders achieve their effectiveness mainly through the stories they tell. In addition to communicating stories, however, Gardner believes that leaders must embody those stories:

> Stories have identity. [They are] narratives that help people think about and feel who they are, where they come from, and where they are headed. [They] constitute the … single most powerful weapon in the leader's arsenal.[9]

So, the real question for you as a leader is: do you possess sufficient self-reliance to author a distinctive story — or at least a chapter — in the life of your organisation or business unit? Does the story engage people and provide them with a relevant and potent dream? Can you do this for your customers and, more importantly, can you then empower them to realise those dreams by buying into the vision, product or service that you are responsible for providing?

Strategy two — self-belief

So far we've talked about leadership as acting and leadership as storytelling. But real leadership is about something more. Once you have accepted responsibility for authoring your vision and have made this vision visible to your people, it's about belief in your ability to realise that dream. In other words, if self-reliance is the most important emotional platform for building independence, then self-belief is the energy that drives the leadership engine. Do you remember the prerequisite for leading the cavalry charge? You've got to believe you look great on that horse!

I concur with leadership guru Tom Peters, who believes that a problem with most books on leadership is that they focus on tactics and motivation (and, frankly, manipulation). Sure, leadership is all about doing, and doing things well, but your ability to lead well depends on the strength of your convictions — particularly those about yourself. This means that you need a psychology of leadership. You have to have confidence in your judgement and be willing to back yourself, putting yourself on the line to achieve your objectives.

The quest for personal power

What does a psychology of leadership come down to? After more than a quarter of a century of studying how people make their best choices, seize opportunities, generate lasting motivation, maintain energetic mood states and develop resilience to adversity and stress, psychologists are almost unanimous that most of it depends on how much self-efficacy you possess.

Put simply, self-efficacy is about how much belief you have in your ability to exercise control over your own behaviour and over events that affect your life. In other words, how much personal power you feel you possess really depends on the degree to which you perceive you are in control of what is happening and can influence the outcome. How stressed and vulnerable you feel is dependent on the degree to which you feel you are not in control, or controlled by external factors, such as other people or situations.

If you think about your personal and professional life, you will find that the areas in which you experience the greatest sense of power and satisfaction are the areas in which you feel you have the greatest amount of control, or ability to exert influence, over what is going on.

A strong sense of self-efficacy enhances your capacity to lead well. It enables you to approach difficult tasks as challenges to be mastered rather than as threats to be avoided. It enables you to set challenging goals and maintain a strong commitment to them. In short, you must have a robust sense of efficacy to sustain the effort needed to overcome challenging circumstances and succeed. As Bruce Barton said, 'Nothing splendid has ever been achieved except by those who dared believe that something inside them was superior to circumstance'.

Genuine self-belief comes from deep inside yourself. It is not a superficial attitude. It goes with a certain ability to dig deep inside yourself and become aware of what you really want, and then making a commitment to gain deliberate control over the process of making those ideas a reality. Self-efficacy beliefs determine how you feel, think, motivate yourself and behave.

So, where do you get it? Well, there are four main sources.

Mastery — value what you do

The first source of self-efficacy involves mastery experiences. Each success you experience builds a robust belief in your self-efficacy. They accumulate to convince you that you have what it takes. That's why it is so critical that you regularly remind yourself of your positive efforts and reward yourself for them. Confirming your progress by celebrating your successes and acknowledging your efforts renews your energy and provides the motivational lift to keep you moving forwards towards your goals. Do it purposefully and regularly!

In addition to recalling past successes, another way to boost your sense of mastery is to picture the positive performance you want. Every achievement and every product created (including you) begins as a vision — an idea in someone's mind. Vision sets the process in motion. Visualise yourself as the extraordinarily competent leader you imagine yourself being. The thoughts and images that you repeatedly focus on have a remarkable way of becoming your reality. This is not trite, pop psychology. After all, it was William James, one of the most respected psychologists in recent times, who commented that 'there is a law in psychology that if you form a picture in your mind of what you would like to be, and you keep and hold that picture there long enough, you will soon become exactly as you have been thinking'. Sharpen the picture of the kind of leader you aspire to be and focus on it daily.

Modelling — seeing is believing

The second source of self-efficacy is modelling. Seeing people similar to yourself succeed by sustained effort increases your belief that you, too, possess the capabilities to master similar skills and challenges. Think about it for a minute. How often do you compare yourself with others and find yourself evaluating your own achievements in light of the choices and achievements of others? Modelling is a powerful way to develop your self-efficacy. The people that you most admire and look up to have a powerful influence on how you think and feel about yourself and the kind of decisions you make. Select some key people who you consider lead well and consider the similarities between yourself and them. Then ask yourself how they would handle a situation. What would they do? Determine to model your response on theirs. This will shape your skill set in this area.

MODELLING IS A POWERFUL WAY TO DEVELOP YOUR SELF-EFFICACY

Mentoring — listening to trusted advisers

The third source of self-efficacy comes from the effect that other people have on you. The more you are persuaded by trusted advisers that you possess the capabilities to master the challenges of leadership, the more likely you are to mobilise your efforts to develop the skills you need to succeed. This implies that you are receptive to others.

The more genuinely receptive you are to the contribution of others, and the more you appreciate their value, the more their contribution will increase in your life. Often our emotions can cloud our judgement about our actual talents. If you are unsure about your natural talent and ability, then ask someone who knows you well what he or she thinks your signature strengths really are. People who know you well can act as trusted advisers and provide you with valuable insights.

One of the most powerful ways to gather this information is to obtain an objective assessment by completing a psychometric evaluation of your emotional intelligence. The Emotional Capital Inventory is the world's first tool specifically designed to measure emotional intelligence and leadership. I've found this to be one of the most effective methods for empowering individuals and building self-efficacy. Identifying both your signature strengths and development areas puts you back in control of your development and greatly accelerates your capacity to succeed.

Mood — if it feels good, do it!

The fourth source of self-efficacy may be surprising to some. It comes from the feedback you receive from your emotional and physical experience. These experiences shape your mood, and your mood affects your judgements about your personal efficacy. A positive mood enhances your self-efficacy.

This is where emotional intelligence is so important. If you are not fully aware of what emotions you are feeling and how it affects you, you lose a crucial piece of feedback to inform your actions. Research on emotional intelligence has taught us that thoughts and feelings, cognitions and emotions, work together to create action. And for the simple reason that thoughts determine feelings and actions, a number of psychological and philosophical traditions, such as Buddhism, emphasise 'right thinking' as a path to maturity and freedom.

It works like this. What you believe, combined with what you are feeling, determines your reality. Your mood is not as remote from your control as you sometimes feel it is. You can think yourself into happiness or depression. You can think yourself into peace of mind or anger. You can think yourself into a restricted, limited world characterised by procrastination and impulsivity, or you can think yourself into a creative life where your choices create products, solve problems and create value. It all depends on what your brain habitually focuses on. As Emerson said, 'thoughts rule the world'. So, the challenge is to train your brain to continually focus on your signature strengths and the opportunities for self-development inherent in most situations.

Now, admittedly, it takes practice. But to stop believing in yourself by allowing your negative mood to determine your behaviour is so damaging to your happiness, wellbeing and leadership authority that nothing could possibly be worth it. Learning to recognise and be aware of your emotions will enable you to pause and take care of your thoughts. Your feelings and actions will take care of themselves. I discuss this in more detail in chapter 4.

The four-minute manager

Let's put all this together. Quite recently, I was listening to Roger Bannister speak at celebrations for the fiftieth anniversary of a remarkable achievement — the breaking of the four-minute mile.

In 1954, the entire sports world believed that it was humanly impossible to run a mile in under four minutes. This limiting belief was supported by research reported in more than fifty medical journals throughout the world that attested to the 'fact'. Of course, we now know that Bannister challenged and broke through that barrier. What is not well known is that within the eighteen months following Bannister's accomplishment, the four-minute mile was achieved by more than forty-five runners. It is difficult to believe that technical training techniques changed so dramatically in that short amount of time that it resulted in making the goal attainable. It's more likely that once the four-minute barrier was broken, all those runners believed it could be broken again.

SELF-BELIEF IS THE MATCH THAT LIGHTS THE FIRE OF CREATIVE ENTHUSIASM AMONG YOUR PEOPLE

This is a clear illustration of the sources of self-efficacy I've been describing. Those forty-five athletes had a vision that they were capable of mastering the four-minute mile. Roger Bannister modelled the successful performance they were seeking to achieve. No doubt their mentors and coaches provided them with the necessary positive feedback regarding their signature strengths. But it was what had changed in their neuropsychology — their emotional brain — that made the critical difference. Once they could feel it in their bones — at the level of their emotions, physiology and mood — the world changed. The rest is history!

Come on baby light my fire

Self-belief is ultimately important for leadership because it is the match that lights the fire of creative enthusiasm among your people. It's exactly the same with leadership. More than knowledge or technical excellence, it is your self-belief expressed as independent creative initiative that is the catalyst that ignites action.

Just as your level of self-belief has a dramatic impact on your leadership effectiveness, so, too, does the self-belief of the people who work in and around your business affect their productivity. The same sources that build your self-efficacy, also build your team's self-efficacy. Growing others involves developing their self-efficacy through mastery, modelling, mentoring and mood.

Building emotional capital

Supporting mastery experiences entails creating a supportive leadership climate where people are given opportunities for participation and involvement; where assumptions can be questioned, innovation is encouraged; and where the tasks provided are challenging. This climate should be supported by a leadership style designed to model emotionally intelligent behaviours that command trust and respect. Once you demonstrate that you are ready to take personal risks, you will display a high degree of self-efficacy. This impacts upon your people by inspiring them to take risks through innovation and initiative. I discuss both these approaches in much closer detail in chapter 7.

Your role as leader also involves you positioning yourself as coach or mentor. Mentoring your people will produce outstanding performance.

Okay, so you 'don't have time'. To build emotional capital you must make time, particularly with your high-potential people. The mentoring and coaching relationship creates an ongoing conversation that provides people with performance feedback that encourages the development of their self-efficacy. At the very least, make sure you have personal conversations with your people and provide individual coaching for as many as you can. This communicates that you value them as individuals and are committed to supporting their aspirations.

Lastly, Goleman's latest research demonstrates that a leader's mood is contagious. Once you have mastered how to develop and maintain a positive mood at work, infect as many people as you can! Offer a convincing vision and attractive goals linked to material rewards. Display your optimism and continually encourage your people by providing positive feedback and offering them opportunities for personal and professional growth. An upbeat mood conveys a 'can do' attitude.

Summary

The journey to becoming an emotional capitalist starts with accepting responsibility for yourself and your leadership role. It is essential that you decide to believe in the value of who you are and what you have to offer. Once you make this decision the emotional centres of your brain release an emotional energy that motivates you to lead as if what you are doing is the most important thing in the world.

All organisations need people like this — individuals who can articulate a shared idea of why they exist, who they are and where they are going. There remains a continual need for leaders who are self-reliant and independent at their core. Men and women with solid levels of self-reliance and self-belief are emotionally independent, which means they can formulate and clarify vision and values and leverage the talent of others to achieve their full potential. Developing and expressing independence enables you to become the catalyst that drives the change you want to see in your business.

Today, providing direction is no longer a matter of command and control—and leaders who are still busy telling people what to do have already ceased to lead. Instead, leadership means accepting responsibility for providing a focus that allows and encourages people to concentrate on what really matters. Emotional capitalists exercise emotional management rather than micro-management. In a fast-paced and pressured working world, people call out for individuals who are independent and can stand above the chaos and provide a coherent story for their professional lives.

Developing self-reliance is the starting point of unlocking your potential and achieving more than you ever have. The next six chapters build on this platform and describe the essential competencies for accomplishing more through your leadership than you thought possible.

Building emotional capital

Strategies for developing self-reliance

Make a declaration of independence from being judged by the estimation of others and decide to take responsibility for accomplishing something unique — decide you look good on that horse!

☑ Get up off the slab, become self-reliant and accept personal responsibility for being the creative force in every area of your personal and professional life.

☑ Remind yourself that you are a leader and have been called to do the work of leadership — act the part.

☑ Become the 'chief storytelling officer' by regularly repeating the story of what the business is trying to achieve, and emphasise how each person fits into the big picture.

☑ Provide a description of why the group must change, where it is going and how it will get there.

☑ Suspend judgement of yourself and develop your personal power through self-efficacy beliefs.

☑ Build your self-efficacy by celebrating small wins, recognising small achievements and commemorating milestones — all the time.

☑ Model yourself on leaders you admire, identify your signature strengths by listening to trusted advisers, eradicate negative thoughts and build positive mood by practising right thinking.

☑ Become a four-minute manager by:

- providing your people with opportunities to develop mastery experiences and model emotionally intelligent behaviours

- mentoring high-potential employees by taking every opportunity to inject self-confidence into those who have earned it

- displaying your optimism and conveying an upbeat mood.

This above all: to thine own self be true,
And it must follow, as the night the day,
Thou canst not then be false to any man.

William Shakespeare

To know oneself, one should assert oneself.

Albert Camus

3 Assertiveness

Another of the emotional skills from the studies of high-performing leaders on which they scored well was assertiveness. Of course, as a number of commentators point out, while you wouldn't expect high-performing leaders to be shrinking violets, the aggressive, bullying boss is definitely out of style. In contrast to being aggressive or passive, assertiveness involves being able to communicate your message honestly and directly, while respecting the fact that others may hold a different opinion or expectation. In other words, when used in leadership, assertiveness really involves two competencies. The first competency involves giving clear messages that help people focus on what needs to be done. Of course, this is difficult to do if your mind is fogged with anxiety and worry. These experiences will bias what you think and say and produce defensive reactions such as dominating others or defaulting to people's agenda. To communicate clearly

55

and consistently requires a second emotional competency, self-control. Developing control over your emotions enables you to manage anxiety and establish a calm mind and authoritative presence. It involves understanding and focusing your attention on the things you can control — your own thoughts, feelings and actions, and letting go of the things you can't control — what other people think, say and do.

Assertive leaders have high expectations of themselves and their people, and possess a reassuring self-confidence. They provide clear directions, feedback and encouragement. They respond to their people's needs and, therefore, create buy-in for their messages. They also manage their emotions, maintaining a calm yet authoritative presence used to resolve conflict and negotiate positive outcomes for all stakeholders associated with the business.

Strategy one — give clear messages

As I suggested in chapter 2, leadership will almost always involve providing a strong vision of the future; a strong set of values by which to operate; a clear purpose; and a sense of being available when asked. By demonstrating these behaviours consistently, you create emotional and intellectual capital.

People want clear leadership that inspires, rather than leadership that bores, or, worse, dominates them. Leadership actually stops being effective when it constitutes simply telling others what to do, or even when it means merely settling for consensus. Instead, it's always been about providing direction and, increasingly, about stimulating colleagues to be individually creative. This involves knowing them as customers.

Assertiveness, then, is more than simply managing conflict. At its most effective it's a communications strategy driven by the principles of effective marketing — it aims to sell a message.

Honesty's the best policy

You've heard it said that, 'The way to a man's heart is through his stomach'. In other words, the very best way to sell your message to others is by responding to their needs. What this means is that when you communicate, always craft your message with a focus on meeting the fundamental needs of other people.

What are those needs?

Generally, in the workplace today, people have a great need for honesty, respect, appreciation and recognition. Communicating in an honest, straightforward manner is the first and most basic platform upon which assertive communication is built.

The medium is the message

Being honest and straightforward communicates your values in ways that uniquely represent who you are. Deeply held values provide the confidence for authentic self-assertion. They define an enduring code of conduct and are the rules of engagement in the process of communicating your message. If Marshall McLuhan was right, and the 'medium is the message', then the medium is you. The words themselves are not enough. Your message has to be a genuine expression of yourself. If your vision is disingenuous, people sense it. Boldt reminds us that electrical engineers measure resistance in terms of ohms. In human relations, resistance is measured in degrees of trust — or rather, the lack of it. To become a credible leader, first you have to recognise the values, beliefs and assumptions that drive you, and communicate a message that is consistent with them.

I recently met with Joe Collins, the state finance manager for a large beverage company. Joe had the unenviable brief to present the new organisational model to his state team. At the previous week's national executive conference he listened to the board and CEO expound the virtues of the new direction — such as cost savings, the benefits of managing fewer resources and greater efficiencies. While he could see the facts for himself, this well-rehearsed 'good story' didn't address the issue he knew the general staff would focus on — what the changes would mean to them. The unspoken part of the equation involved the challenges the new model would present to staff — that is, the anxiety and discomfort of yet another restructure and the potential loss of jobs. These were factors that mattered to Joe and he knew that to be true to his own values they would need to be at the top of his agenda when speaking with his team. He knew that only through being genuine and open, and by respecting his team by at least acknowledging the tough issues, could he hope to carry them with him.

In other words, for Joe to sell the message of the new direction to his people he first had to market the idea to them. He recognised that he must take account of both his customers' needs, particularly their need for clarity and security, and the potential benefits that the new direction would bring to them. This would increase the likelihood of them buying into his message.

Joe's experience demonstrates that assertiveness as a strategy for communication, is most effective when driven by three principles of effective marketing: document your position; acknowledge your customers' needs; and acknowledge emotional contracts.

Document your position

The first principle involves documenting your position. Before communicating your message, be clear about the message you want to deliver and ensure it is aligned with your values. As I've already suggested, a leader's views must represent things they deeply care about. In this way he or she will have emotional power and lasting motivation to draw from. Know what you want and why it's important to you and to others before you speak. This equips you with the ability to document your position before you ask others to agree to your views and adopt them. People will listen to leaders who hold strong beliefs about matters of principle and demonstrate a willingness to stand up for their beliefs. In other words, if they don't believe the messenger they won't believe the message.

Acknowledge your customers' needs

The second principle of marketing your message involves recognising where the value lies for your customers. People have a fundamental need to understand what's in it for them. Assertive communication is not to be confused with being a corporate megaphone. Leaders who rely on aggressive, top–down communication hardly ever move beyond 'tell' and 'sell', and almost never get to 'buy', let alone the 'buy into' stage. At the end of the day, all good communication is really an attempt to get people to buy into your message, whether it's standing your ground on a matter of principle, dealing with conflict, delivering critical feedback or actively advocating for a personal position or a group of people.

Your aim is always to deliver an outcome. This outcome is best achieved when the other party buys into what you are selling. And, like all good marketing strategies, sales are more easily achieved when you respond to your customers' needs.

ASSERTIVE COMMUNICATION IS NOT TO BE CONFUSED WITH BEING A CORPORATE MEGAPHONE

Always keep in mind how important it is to take the time to genuinely acknowledge that you understand the other person's position or the potential impact that the action may have on him or her. This will also involve including, wherever possible, a 'benefit statement', which focuses on the potential benefit of the action for the customer. Your customers are far more likely to buy into your position when they feel there has been an honest attempt to respond to their needs.

Joe's actions highlighted this in the way he undertook the change process with his team. He knew that to maximise their buy-in they needed to be involved in creating the transition plan. Joe developed a three-stage plan. Initially he sought their feedback on the restructure. Rather than just asking their opinions, he also outlined that their feedback would form the basis for the second stage. At the second stage they were given the responsibility to outline what they needed to assist them in making the transition workable for themselves. Stage three would see the team implementing their plan. By allowing his people to have a voice and giving them scope to tailor the process to meet their operational needs, he was encouraging each person to have ownership over the new direction. Rather than the transition being something that they were subjected to, Joe created buy-in by making his people part of the new direction.

Acknowledge emotional contracts

The third marketing principle that supports assertive communication involves recognising and acknowledging the emotional contract operating between people. Emotional contracts are really the unwritten set of expectations and assumptions that hold people in relationship with other people and the organisation. These expectations usually involve the psychological and emotional connections, such as trust, confidence and empathy. Emotionally intelligent leaders aim to create strong emotional contracts between individuals and the organisation, and they recognise that it is what people hold in their hearts — emotional capital — that matters most in determining the effectiveness of their message.

This implies that to be effective, assertive communication involves communicating your values and feelings and acknowledging the feelings of the person receiving the message. By putting people in the picture, and by demonstrating that you understand something of their experience, you leverage the emotional contract between you and your people and create a receptive frame of mind for your message.

I hear you saying, 'This is getting a bit soft. I get the bit about being a straight shooter and even the bit about adding a benefit statement, but, acknowledging emotional contracts?' Well, remember my comment on the relationship between hearts and stomachs earlier. Selling a message to customers is all about providing them with emotional gratification. This doesn't mean that you simply 'suck up' to customers. What it does mean is that you craft your message in such a way that it ties into the most emotionally gratifying elements of a customer's needs. For example, Heinz Kohut, an eminent psychologist, pointed out that people are ultimately motivated by one of two fundamental emotional needs: the need to be admired or the need to be understood. For the most part, people have a fundamental need to be understood and it's this that often forms the basis of the emotional contract. By taking the time to communicate that you understand a person's experience, you establish a level of common ground that overcomes resistance and forms the basis of becoming receptive to you and your ideas.

Building emotional capital

When you get down to basics, assertive communication is about providing clear messages that capture the hearts and minds of people. This involves expressing your views in an authentic way that leaves no-one in doubt about your values. It includes documenting your position by recalling the facts and taking the time to genuinely acknowledge that you understand the other person's position and the benefit to him or her. Finally, you need to communicate your values and feelings openly while acknowledging and supporting the feelings of those receiving your message.

Strategy two — self-control

All very well, but the trick to behaving assertively is to control your negative feelings. But where do your feelings come from? Typically, we have two mechanisms that we use to deal with confrontation: we can fight it or we can flee from it. This is called the 'flight or fight' response. It is an automatic physical response designed to enable us to take rapid action when confronted by physical threat.

Are you aware of your own power and the effect you have on others? Are you secure enough to empower others? Do you take full responsibility for that power? Do you ever feel intimidated? Do you maintain your sense of self-confidence when you are with people who seem better educated, more eloquent, or more accomplished than you are? Do you sometimes feel your power sapping away as you walk to the front of the room to address senior people in your organisation?

It's the feeling of not being in control that ultimately causes people to feel a lack of freedom and to feel trapped or vulnerable. This triggers negative emotions, such as anger, frustration and anxiety. Negative emotions are the primary causes not only of underachievement and failure, but also of bullying and passivity. The elimination of these destructive emotions is the number one job for the person who aspires to lead others and communicate clear, positive messages.

Every destructive emotion that we experience as adults, we had to learn. It starts in childhood through the process of imitation, practice, repetition and reinforcement. And, since negative emotions are learned, like most things, they can be unlearned and their effect on your behaviour minimised.

Emotional highjacker — anxiety

We all know something about anxiety. At its most basic level anxiety is really about the feeling of losing control. Again, it's possible to trace this feeling back to your early development. As a young person you depended on others to supply the things you needed. To ensure a reliable supply it's highly likely that you developed various ways of controlling your suppliers — such as tantrums, sulking, shouting or stubborn resistance. Given that these tactics failed to deliver the full control you were looking for, you were probably left feeling a little out of control. As a reaction to these feelings, you formed coping patterns that you likely carried into adulthood.

ANXIETY IS REALLY ABOUT THE FEELING OF LOSING CONTROL

Dominating

One of the most common coping patterns is to display dominance by becoming a 'control freak'. The more you try to exert control and be 'in charge', only to fail, the more out of control or anxious you feel. As situations become more pressured, the more anxious you feel and the more you try to control. All of these attempts to control what are essentially uncontrollable factors — external circumstances and the feelings, thoughts and behaviour of others — lead to exaggerated attempts to regain control through dominating others.

A couple of years ago I was coaching Paul, who'd set himself up as a management consultant. Paul felt most in control when he could order his environment by making solo decisions, managing his own projects and determining his own working hours. This worked when he was a sole operator, but when he hired his first employee, Tim, this preferred style became counterproductive. While logically he knew he couldn't exert this level of control over Tim, emotionally he hung on to this style even as he saw its negative impact. The more Paul felt his power slipping, the greater his focus on Tim's every action and decision. He asked to be briefed on Tim's diary every morning, consulted on Tim's every decision and contact, and he wanted to be present at all client meetings. What Paul failed to see was that in attempting to control Tim's every move he was giving himself twice the work, alienating his employee and potentially creating problems with clients. Curiously, the more Paul frantically tried to stabilise his environment, the more out of control and anxious he felt.

Defaulting

At the other end of the spectrum of coping behaviour for managing anxiety is defaulting to others. When we are anxious about being judged or rejected by others we may default to their view or position to avoid conflict. This is really an effort to preserve a sense of control by remaining emotionally distant. Appearing passive and acquiescing to others avoids the anxiety associated with being responsible for our own views and decisions, or, at least, for having to deal with the added pressure that conflict creates.

I recently met Rachel, who had taken over the position of head of international finance for a large Asian bank. After agreeing to take on more projects than anyone else on her team in a short-sighted attempt to prove her commitment, Rachel was quickly drowning under the workload and feeling increasing pressure. Her tendency when feeling overwhelmed was to limit as many distractions as possible, and this was illustrated at the monthly board meeting. Rather than voicing her usually insightful and valuable views on an upcoming proposal, she remained silent. She chose instead to defer to her colleagues, even though she disagreed with most of their views. By not having to prepare an amended proposal, this undoubtedly saved her time in the short term. But it actually created the long-term frustration of having to live with, and make operational, a decision she did not believe in, and one that was ultimately unworkable. While in the previous scenario, Paul was trying to control his world by being too involved, Rachel had the opposite problem — she was trying to stay in control by using avoidance.

Building emotional capital

In contrast to being dominating and aggressive, and to defaulting and being passive, assertive communication involves being able to manage your own anxiety as well as potential or actual conflict by being able to communicate your message honestly and directly. Imagine you've been putting in late nights working on the tender for a multi-site contract. It is a joint project, but your colleague has not completed his sections even though the draft was due to be submitted to the executive team that morning. Furthermore, he did not attend the tender briefing with you, and you have had to spend precious time explaining the brief to him. You are both equally experienced so this is not about ability. He's spoken about relationship problems and most days he has lengthy telephone calls with his wife. You would like to be supportive, but frankly you are becoming increasingly frustrated, and you realise that you are doing most of the work. In addition, your anxiety levels are mounting because the deadline has come and gone.

You have a choice between three strategies: dominance, defaulting or assertiveness. Dominance means you could drop your bundle and confront your colleague aggressively, pointing out his irresponsible actions and demanding that he get his act together, now! Alternatively, defaulting involves you quietly sitting and fuming about his apparent thoughtlessness, working harder, and cringing inwardly when both of you are praised for a job well done. The third strategy, assertiveness, means acting in an emotionally intelligent way and communicating your message honestly and directly, while respecting the fact that he may have a different view of the situation or hold different expectations. The third approach is more likely to result in both you and the other party achieving your objectives.

Be clear about what you want and take responsibility for your own feelings. Remember that they are your feelings and nobody can make you feel mad, bad or sad without your permission.

BE CLEAR ABOUT WHAT YOU WANT AND TAKE RESPONSIBILITY FOR YOUR OWN FEELINGS

As the Gestalt prayer reminds us, you are not here to live up to other peoples' expectations and they are not here to live up to yours.

This means you can choose to stay in control of your feelings and approach your colleague in a rational and calm manner. Establish direct eye contact and stay in close proximity. Use a neutral tone of voice, not allowing your voice to become too loud. Begin by documenting your position. Acknowledge that you understand something of his position. Communicate your feelings of frustration and anxiety to him or her regarding the situation and invite his response. If in his response he does not acknowledge a problem or a commitment to a solution, reinforce your point of view again — use the 'broken record' approach in which you repeat what it is you want. Finally, work with him to achieve a compromised solution.

Certainly, assertiveness is more challenging, but it is the emotionally intelligent option. It reinforces self-respect and increases interpersonal awareness and greatly increases your stocks of emotional capital.

Summary

I can hear you asking, 'Where do I start?'

You start by understanding that in terms of emotional intelligence, assertiveness is fundamentally a communications strategy driven by marketing principles. In other words, it's not just about finding middle ground between being aggressive or passive. And it's not just about managing conflict. It's about doing an effective job of selling your ideas and views to all of your customers, even when they don't agree with them or actively resist them. To do this you have to use a marketing strategy that considers the minds of your customers.

You begin by understanding that conflict and resistance — as well as your own anxiety about losing control — are largely the result of unmet emotional needs in people. It's these emotional needs that not only fuel resistance and defensive responding, but ultimately provide the powerful drive for productive cooperation. Establishing a platform of trust by communicating your message honestly and directly, while respecting the fact that others may hold a different opinion or expectation, involves documenting your position. You do this by recalling the facts, taking the time to genuinely acknowledge that you understand the other person's position, and then focusing on the benefit to him or her. It also involves recognising that the impulse for emotional gratification (and buying!) is more powerful than a person's rational needs alone. This means acknowledging the emotional contracts that underlie every rational need. In this way, you focus on what is likely to provide emotional gratification for the customer and avoid what may trigger its opposite — emotional resistance.

Of course, this also involves the ability to control your own negative emotional reactions to customer resistance and hostility. Rather than responding by dominating or defaulting to others, acknowledge the right of others to disagree and take responsibility for your own emotional choices.

Let's not forget that assertiveness is built on the platform established in chapter 2 — self-reliance. Successful leadership is not a matter of command and control, but, rather, about communicating your vision clearly and consistently towards a shared ideal while maintaining effective control of your emotional capital. This enables you to provide direction and keep your people headed towards their goals. It's fundamentally about being able to mobilise everyone around you and move everyone's imagination forwards. Developing and expanding this attitude is the challenge of becoming an optimistic leader — the subject of the next chapter.

Building emotional capital

Strategies for developing assertiveness

- ☑ Communicate in an honest, straightforward manner, and be consistent.

- ☑ Communicate a strong vision of the future, a strong set of values by which to operate, a clear purpose and a sense of being available when asked.

- ☑ Know what you want and why it's important to you and to others before you speak.

- ☑ Acknowledge the emotional contract in each relationship by pausing to recognise and understand the feelings of others.

- ☑ Stay in control of your feelings and approach people in a rational and calm manner.

- ☑ Become aware of your anxiety and tendency to dominate or default and take responsibility for your own feelings and what you want.

- ☑ Establish direct eye contact and use a neutral tone of voice.

- ☑ Document your position by recalling the facts.

- ☑ Take time to genuinely acknowledge that you understand the other person's position and include, wherever possible, a 'benefit statement' for the customer.

Human beings can alter their lives by altering their attitude of mind.

William James

The great secret to going through life is as a person who never gets used to failing.

Albert Schweitzer

4 Optimism

Optimism is perhaps the most important quality you can develop to achieve greater success as a leader. Generating scores almost one standard deviation above the average in all of our leadership studies, optimism differentiates high-performing leaders from the rest. Not just 'the glass is half full' kind of optimism, but optimism as a strategy — a way of dealing with difficulties and sensing opportunities.

Optimistic leaders can see the big picture and have a vision of where they are going. They are characterised by three attitudes. First, they look for the benefit in every situation, especially when they experience setbacks. No matter what happens, they are committed to finding answers and possess a confident expectation of success. Second, optimists seek the valuable lesson in every problem or difficulty. Rather than focusing all energy on the deal just lost, the optimist thinks about what to do differently the next time around. Third, optimistic leaders focus on the task to be accomplished rather than on negative emotions such as disappointment or fear. They see the possibilities within the task. Jack Welch puts it succinctly when he says:

> *Your job as leader is to fight the gravitational pull of negativism. That doesn't mean you sugarcoat the challenges your team faces. It does mean you get out of your office and into everyone's skin, really caring about what they're doing and how they're faring as you take the hill together.*[10]

Optimism and resilience in the face of adversity are the greatest long-term predictors of success for individuals and organisations. An overwhelming body of research demonstrates that optimists perform better at work, regularly outperform the predictions of aptitude tests, have greater resistance to colds and other illnesses, and they recover faster from illness and injury. Optimists also make considerably more money!

Smile and the world smiles with you

You've heard it said, 'A picture's worth a thousand words'. Photographs, in particular, have a power to capture in a fleeting second what is true of many other moments in life as well.

'Say cheese', the photographer tells you, and you put on your best smile. Psychologists have found that there are actually two kinds of smiles. The first, a Duchenne smile, is authentic. The muscles that produce this are very difficult to control voluntarily so it's produced spontaneously when people are genuinely happy and feeling positive and optimistic. To produce this smile you must actually feel genuinely positive and pleased, before these emotions can be reflected in your facial expression. The other smile, called a Pan American smile (remember the airline?), is disingenuous and plastic. It's produced on demand when the occasion demands that you perform politely.

When experienced psychologists look through photo albums they can tell instantly who are the Duchenne and non-Duchenne smilers.

Sometime ago I was studying at the University of California, Berkeley, when researchers looked at 141 senior-class photos from the 1960 Mills College yearbook.[11] In these photos all but three of the women were smiling, and half of those smiling reflected a Duchenne smile.

Each of these women had been contacted at ages twenty-seven, forty-three and fifty-two, and asked about their marriages and their life satisfaction. Surprisingly, researchers found that the women with the Duchenne smiles, on average, were more likely to be married and remain married, and to experience more personal wellbeing over the next thirty years.

A person with a genuine smile, it turned out, was simply more likely to be doing better. The genuine smile seems to reflect an attitude to life and a high level of optimism that convincingly predicts greater levels of satisfaction.

Optimism delivers success

Psychologist Martin Seligman, former president of the American Psychological Association, spent several years studying the relationship between optimistic thinking and sales success with a large group of Metropolitan Life Insurance Company salespeople. As you can imagine, selling life insurance is considered one of the most difficult of all sales jobs. The company was spending millions of dollars on training sales agents; however, most of them moved on after a few months in the job. Seligman suggested that they hire people with high levels of optimism. When scores were matched to actual sales records, it turned out that agents who scored in the top half for optimism sold 37 per cent more insurance over two years than those in the pessimistic bottom half. Even more interesting, agents who scored in the top 10 per cent for optimism sold 88 per cent more than those ranked in the most pessimistic 10 per cent. Their high levels of optimism meant that they were able to deal better with nine out of 10 rejections. Agents who scored in the bottom 50 per cent on the same test were twice as likely to leave their jobs as their more optimistic colleagues, while the bottom 25 per cent were three times as likely to quit.

Individuals and organisations who view their setbacks in the context of progress are much more likely to continue in their efforts towards success. Your ability to deal with disappointment in a positive, constructive way will do more to enable you to succeed and say more about you to other people than any other single factor. Emotional capitalists are invariably those who have developed the ability to respond constructively to crises and challenges. They are resilient and have skills that enable them to see the opportunities over the horizon even when the next crisis is just ahead.

EMOTIONAL CAPITALISTS ARE INVARIABLY THOSE WHO HAVE DEVELOPED THE ABILITY TO RESPOND CONSTRUCTIVELY TO CRISES AND CHALLENGES

Emotional spin doctor — explanatory style

Many psychologists suggest that 95 per cent of your emotions are determined by the way you talk to yourself. Seligman also spent many years clinically testing the idea of 'learned helplessness'.[12] His experiments with mild electric shocks to dogs proved that two out of three dogs would give up trying to escape if they believed that whatever they did the shocks would keep coming. Another researcher tested the principle on people, using noise instead of shocks, and found that learned helplessness can be created in the minds of people just as easily. Yet, as with the experiments, one in every three human subjects would not 'give up'. They kept trying to press buttons on the panel in an attempt to shut off the noise.

What made these people different from the others? Seligman found that the ability of some people to bounce back from setback is not due to a 'triumph of the will' (as we thought) or due to having some inborn greatness, but, rather, the way people explained events to themselves — their 'explanatory style'. In other words, when things go wrong, do you explain events in terms of your own fundamental incapacity, thereby demotivating yourself and forestalling future attempts to succeed, or do you spin your interpretation of events in such a way as to encourage learning, adaptation and renewed efforts at success?

The difference between being paralysed by setbacks and bouncing back is, more often than not, how you explain the events happening to you and around you — your explanatory style. Optimistic people tend to explain their problems and challenges as transient, controllable and specific to one situation. Pessimistic people, in contrast, believe that their problems last forever, undermine everything they do and are uncontrollable. What Seligman found was that there are three crucial dimensions to your explanatory style: permanence, pervasiveness and personalisation.

Permanence

People who give up easily believe the causes of the bad events that happen to them are permanent — that these causes are always going to be there and affect their lives. They say things to themselves such as 'diets never work' or 'the boss is a bastard'. People who are optimistic and resist helplessness believe these negative events are only temporary. In other words, when something goes wrong optimistic people always explain the event or experience to themselves as though it were a temporary, specific situation, rather than a long-term, general condition. They tell themselves things like 'diets don't work when you eat out' or 'the boss is in a bad mood'. Similarly, when things go well, optimistic people explain things to themselves in terms of permanent causes, such as 'I always fall on my feet'. They view success and happiness as their normal state and see negative events as temporary glitches on the path to inevitable progress.

Pervasiveness

Seligman also found that some people can put their troubles into a box and get on with their lives even when one important aspect of it — their job, for example — is stressful. Others let one problem spill out and affect everything else in their lives — they catastrophise, make universal explanations for their failures and give up on everything when failure strikes in one area. Pessimists tell themselves that 'people are unfair' or 'seminars are a waste of time'; whereas optimists contextualise the situation and provide specific explanations for bad events. Optimists say things to themselves such as 'she was unfair' or 'this seminar is a waste of time'. In other words, optimists view negative events as isolated phenomena, insulated from other areas of their lives. This enables them to bounce back from problems more quickly.

Personalisation

A further aspect of explanatory style is the way people often personalise a situation. When they become discouraged, they will often attach a sense of personal failure to their discouragement: 'If I had done that, this might not have happened'. While introspection is good in times of discouragement, attacking ourselves for circumstances beyond our control is not. When optimists confront misfortune or bad news they react differently. Optimists don't take it personally; they can see the influence of external factors in their problems.

Essentially, Seligman is saying that in the face of misfortune or bad news pessimists focus on the negative and assume it's permanent (it will never change), consider its influence pervasive (it's going to affect everything I do) and take it personally (it's my own fault). By doing this they give up and become paralysed; whereas when your explanations take the opposite form you become energised. In this way, your explanatory style is the critical factor in determining whether you are a positive or negative person.

Strategy one – look for the benefit

The good news is that, although your explanatory style has become a habit over time, you can learn to change this mindset. How you interpret an event is under your control. It is a matter of choice. You determine how you are going to feel and react by how you choose to explain a situation to yourself. Choose to put a positive spin on it, whatever it is. You are in charge.

Optimism – a feeling to be learned

A positive mental attitude can be defined as a constructive response to stress. It doesn't mean that, no matter what happens, you are happy and cheerful all the time. Stress is inevitable—the only thing over which you have any control is how you respond to these stressful events. If you respond in a positive, constructive way, you will maintain a generally positive attitude. When your mind is calm and clear, you will be more creative and alert. You will also be more likely to see alternative ways to solve problems, and keep moving towards accomplishing your goals.

When you respond in a negative or angry way to a problem or difficulty, you trigger a series of nervous reactions that shut down the most creative parts of your brain. Instead of going into a 'react and respond' way of thinking, you develop a 'flight or fight' mentality. You can learn to think and succeed like an optimist by changing your explanatory style, even if you are a confirmed pessimist.

You can even benefit from this mindset when sensing business opportunities. Quite recently, a shoe factory sent two marketing scouts to a region of Africa to study the prospects for business expansion. One sent back a telegram saying, 'Situation hopeless stop no-one wears shoes'. The other wrote back excitedly, 'Glorious business opportunity stop they have no shoes!'

The roots of this experience go much deeper than just attitude or personality. Neuropsychology has taught us that our view of the world is shaped by the selective information that our senses bring us about what is out there. Over time we have learned to pay attention to certain phenomenon and to ignore other things. The brain then constructs its own simulation of the sensations; only at that stage do we have our first conscious experience of what's around us. In other words, just as physical behaviours become habits over time (such as writing style, or even which leg you put into your jeans first!), our emotional responses are also habitual. Our view of the world and our emotional responses to it become a well-formed map. It's a construction of our own making, and with careful attention it can be continually redrawn. Optimism really is a feeling to be learned.

Strategy two — seek the valuable lesson

In addition to looking for the benefit in most situations, the second attitude that characterises optimists is that they tend to seek the valuable lesson in every problem or difficulty.

The moral of the story

In studying the characteristics of the most resilient leaders, I found that one characteristic that generally stands out is the ability to maintain a hopeful attitude by learning from the lessons of a previous experience to improve performance. These individuals have trained themselves to respond to negative situations with the thought, 'What can I learn from this situation that will make me better the next time I face it?'

WHAT CAN I LEARN FROM THIS SITUATION THAT WILL MAKE ME BETTER THE NEXT TIME I FACE IT?

After an important event, both winners and losers examine how they performed. Underachievers almost invariably rehash the mistakes they have made, the expenses they have incurred and the failures they have experienced. Emotional capitalists, by contrast, are those who think positively about themselves and their lives; they are constantly reviewing the best parts of their performance and making plans to repeat those actions again.

Strategy three — focus on the task and see the possibilities

The third attitude that characterises optimistic leaders is that, rather than allow themselves to be clouded by negative emotions, they focus on the task and see the possibilities within the task.

Opportunity knocks

In other words, optimists don't go around maniacally excited about everything or neurotically distressed by problems. Instead, the optimistic leader sees how the job can be done and is logical about it. This is not to be confused with having a technical approach — technical people often tend to focus on the drawbacks. Optimistic leaders, on the other hand, do not focus on the drawbacks, but are instead able to define the problem and see how it can be solved. Your task in becoming an optimistic leader is to convince technical people that because of their technical skills they can solve these problems.

IF YOU CHANGE THE DEFINITION OF A PROBLEM TO A SITUATION, A CHALLENGE OR AN OPPORTUNITY, YOUR RESPONSE TO THE PROBLEM WILL BE POSITIVE

If you change the definition of a problem to a situation, a challenge or an opportunity, your response to the problem will be positive and constructive, rather than negative and angry. If you look at every problem as a potential opportunity, you will almost always find a prospect or benefit that you can take advantage of.

When you experience a disappointment of any kind, your natural reaction is to feel stunned emotionally. You feel as though you have had the wind taken out of you — you feel hurt, let down, disappointed and discouraged. No matter what happened, and no matter how disappointed you are, if you are immediately able to say, 'Every experience is a positive experience if I view it as an opportunity for growth and self-mastery', it will help you control your emotions, thereby building your emotional capital.

Career consultant and personal coach Laurence Boldt reminds us that a patent clerk overcame failure on his college entrance exam and changed our perception of the universe. His name was Albert Einstein. Likewise, a nearly half-deaf man with no more than three weeks formal education overcame his disability and invented motion pictures and the electric light bulb. His name was Thomas Edison. Then, of course, there were a couple of struggling bicycle mechanics named Wilbur and Orville Wright, who inaugurated the era of manned flight.[13]

Optimism is about your vision, foresight and possessing the ability to remain focused on the endgame, despite challenges and setbacks. To become optimistic as a leader you must develop the habit of focusing more on the big picture and communicating realistic confidence in being able to obtain the prize.

Building emotional capital

In addition to looking for the benefit in situations, seeking the valuable lesson in every difficulty, and seeing the possibilities within the task, there are a number of other useful techniques that will help you overcome a pessimistic explanatory style. In this book we will look at three of them, but first let's consider Trevor's situation.

Trevor is a financial planner in a bank. When Trevor heard that Bob Jenson had been appointed as the new branch manager his first thought was it was going to be a disaster. Trevor remembered hearing that at his last branch, Bob had downsized the financial planning department, and within the first month had retrenched three of the existing 10 financial planners. So, quite naturally, Trevor was convinced that if Bob Jenson had downsized a department before, he would do it again, because that is what he always did.

This is a classic example of the way some individuals choose to focus exclusively on what can go wrong. Their explanatory style is based on thinking that catastrophises situations and people. They see the worst-case scenario and attribute a permanent status to nearly every event.

Decatastrophising

To overcome this pessimistic style, Trevor needs to learn to decatastrophise. Decatastrophising is a useful approach for overcoming the explanatory style that attempts to make events negative and permanent rather than temporary. If Trevor was to decatastrophise his thinking, he would realise that Bob Jenson may not necessarily have had downsizing on his mind the moment he stepped in as branch manager. He may also have realised that he needed to wait until he knew Bob Jenson's plan for the branch before assessing the risks to his current employment. This approach would greatly assist him in recognising any opportunities that may emerge, rather than defending himself against possible threat.

Redefining

Trevor's second thought was that when Bob started downsizing he would be the first to go. This was because, in the past, new bosses never seemed to particularly like Trevor until they had worked with him for some time. Once again, Trevor demonstrated the lack of optimism characteristic of individuals who personalise situations excessively. Many people have an explanatory style that frequently personalises situations that can be more readily attributed to external circumstances. Trevor carries a belief that new bosses never like him until they get to know him; he incorporates this thinking into the impersonal event of a new branch manager being appointed. By feeding his negative explanatory style and personalising this event, he allows himself to become even more discouraged. To overcome this pessimistic explanatory style, Trevor needs to learn to redefine the situation. For example, if Trevor was to redefine the situation, he may realise, first of all, that not all of his past managers have actually taken an instant dislike to him. He may conclude that the managers with whom he didn't get on also had the same problem with other people at the beginning and were really quite negative in their initial approach to everyone. In this situation, Trevor could depersonalise his thoughts so that his subsequent feelings about Bob's new appointment are more optimistic.

Disputating

Trevor's third thought was that he would probably have to sell his house because he was unlikely to get a new job at his age and his retrenchment package would never be enough for him to sustain his current lifestyle for an extended period of time. This is an example of how pervasive Trevor's thinking is. He lets one problem spill out and affect everything about his life. Trevor takes a single event, Bob Jenson's appointment, and extrapolates it to a point where he fears he may have to sell the family home. To overcome this pessimistic, pervasive explanatory style, Trevor needs to learn disputation. Disputation is a technique that attempts to identify irrational thinking and replace it with more reasonable thinking.

Irrational thoughts are usually provoked by fears and lead to negative feeling states. If Trevor could recognise the irrational leap in his thinking from getting a new boss to selling the family home, he would then be in a position to choose a more productive way of thinking that would lead to a more optimistic feeling state.

Taken together, these approaches are not wishful thinking or naïve attempts to put on a brave face. They are intelligent, considered approaches to dealing with difficult realities. Decatastrophising, redefining and disputating are actually more reasonable ways of thinking and certainly more useful than automatically succumbing to your emotions. Over time, and with practice, they are the steps for creating an optimistic outlook — and a powerful strategy for building emotional capital in the business.

Summary

When you are faced with a challenging situation, first look for the benefit. Step back from the perceived crisis and recast it not as a catastrophe and a threat, but as a challenge and an opportunity. For example, if it is a brief that you're worrying about, you may focus on the fact that you've written dozens of them before, and that struggling was a necessary part of the process of getting it right. If you're worried about the work of an associate, you might focus on his or her strengths, and take pleasure in the chance to serve as a mentor and pass along your considerable knowledge.

SEEK THE VALUABLE LESSON IN EVERY PROBLEM OR DIFFICULTY

Second, seek the valuable lesson in every problem or difficulty. Remind yourself that by recasting mistakes as lessons, you move from the paralysis of being preoccupied with the past, to a proactive focus on integrating the learning into constructive future action.

Third, let go of the negative emotion that events cause and, instead, focus on the task to be accomplished. In order to feel more secure, you may decide to ask yourself the question: 'What is the worst-case scenario here? If everything that could go wrong did go wrong, could I live with the consequences?' In most cases you'll discover that you can. You can then concentrate on preparing an escape plan, or minimising the consequences if such an event did occur.

Finally, pay more attention to those aspects of your life for which you feel thankful and appreciative — that you have your health, reasonable financial security, your family, or even a job that provides you with the opportunity to exercise your talent and signature strengths.

Your leadership approach is, for want of a better word, contagious. There is a growing body of research on the human brain that demonstrates that a leader's mood and attitude affects the emotions of people around them. Sure, your phsical actions are important, but taken as a whole, the results of psychological and organisational research are conclusive. According to Goleman, 'Emotional leadership is the spark that ignites a company's performance'. As a leader, you need to ensure that you consistently choose an optimistic, authentic approach, and that, through your behaviour, you encourage your people to approach the challenges of the business in the same way.

It is not difficult to imagine why optimism as a strategy — a way of dealing with difficulties and sensing opportunities — translates into strong leadership, sustained motivation and higher performance.

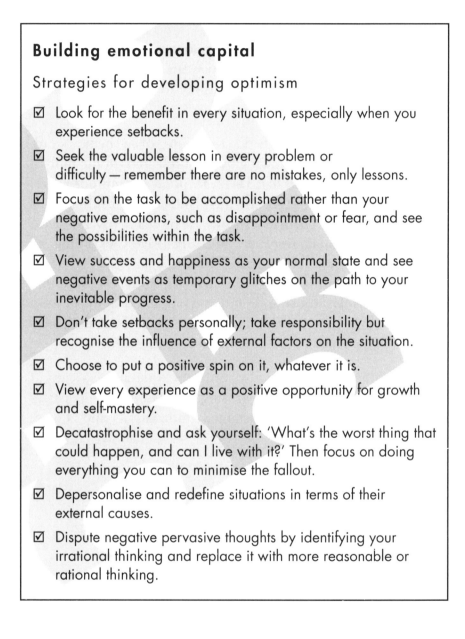

Building emotional capital

Strategies for developing optimism

- ☑ Look for the benefit in every situation, especially when you experience setbacks.
- ☑ Seek the valuable lesson in every problem or difficulty — remember there are no mistakes, only lessons.
- ☑ Focus on the task to be accomplished rather than your negative emotions, such as disappointment or fear, and see the possibilities within the task.
- ☑ View success and happiness as your normal state and see negative events as temporary glitches on the path to your inevitable progress.
- ☑ Don't take setbacks personally; take responsibility but recognise the influence of external factors on the situation.
- ☑ Choose to put a positive spin on it, whatever it is.
- ☑ View every experience as a positive opportunity for growth and self-mastery.
- ☑ Decatastrophise and ask yourself: 'What's the worst thing that could happen, and can I live with it?' Then focus on doing everything you can to minimise the fallout.
- ☑ Depersonalise and redefine situations in terms of their external causes.
- ☑ Dispute negative pervasive thoughts by identifying your irrational thinking and replace it with more reasonable or rational thinking.

Education is not filling a bucket but lighting a fire.

WB Yeats

People are wise in proportion not to their experience, but in their capacity to experience.

George Bernard Shaw

5 Self-actualisation

High-performing leaders in each of our leadership studies produced high scores on the emotional competency of self-actualisation. Interestingly, earlier studies that looked at predictors of success in the workplace found that one factor of emotional intelligence that consistently showed up, almost regardless of job type, was self-actualisation. Nothing is more important to your long-term success as a leader than building your stocks of emotional capital in self-actualisation.

It may sound like a lofty idea only discussed by psychologists in the rarified atmosphere of academia, but in the real world of business there are two components to self-actualisation as a leadership skill. The first involves having a passion for what you do — that is, loving your work and eagerly looking forward to starting each day and taking your business forward. It was the poet WB Yeats who captured this best when he said, 'Education is not filling a bucket but lighting a fire'. The same is true of leadership. More than your technical knowledge, or even your hard work, it is your passion that empowers you to inspire and lead others. You fuel your passion by paying attention to what makes you feel alive and energised — to what interest and excites you.

The second component of self-actualisation involves establishing a work–life balance. None of us can work flat out 24/7 and expect to create anything of lasting value over the long term. If your life is consumed by work, something is missing that is essential to your long-term wellbeing. Ultimately, to become a leader high in self-actualisation you have to have a wide variety of interests and make sure your personal and professional goals are aligned. This creates a reservoir of continual emotional energy — and enduring high performance is not so much about time management as it is about the skillful management of your emotional energy. Every one of your thoughts, emotions and behaviours has an impact on your level of emotional capital — your energy. And physical and emotional capital are inextricably connected. You maximise your emotional capital by making sure that all the important areas of your life get the attention they deserve.

PHYSICAL AND EMOTIONAL CAPITAL ARE INEXTRICABLY CONNECTED

Do what you can do

It was in the summer of 1962 when Abraham Maslow, an academic psychologist, established the Esalen Institute in California, the world's first personal-growth centre. His work centred around the idea of the 'self-actualising person'. Maslow was convinced that people, organisations and cultures have limitless capacity for growth and change. His work became the foundation of a movement in psychology that essentially reimagined what a human being could become.

In his well-known 'hierarchy of needs' theory, Maslow described five basic needs that must be satisfied if you are to survive, find satisfaction and reach your potential. First, you require your basic physical needs — such as food, water and shelter — to be met. Second, you need to achieve safety and be free from threat. Third, you need to feel loved and develop a sense of belonging to a social group. Fourth in the hierarchy is the need for esteem — to have your accomplishments recognised by others and to achieve self-respect. At the top of the pyramid is the fifth need , 'self-actualisation', which Maslow defined simply as, 'one must do what he or she can do'.

Doing what 'you can do', while a very simple thing to say, involves having the wisdom not to accept the roles that others have prescribed for you. Instead, it's about deciding to become the person you know yourself capable of being. As I suggest in chapter 2, your life is like a book with many of the chapters written by other people, providing you with scripts that direct your life. Many people never challenge these scripts and live their entire lives according to the stories hardwired into their emotional brains. A person who accepts leadership is basically someone who decides to take up the pen and author their own experience — write their own chapters, if you like.

Careful though, it takes a certain amount of courage and emotional energy to take up this challenge.

People often approach the challenge of achieving their potential from a 'deficiency motivation', that is, a desire to get more of something that they feel is missing, such as power, social approval, status, money or love. They work hard to be what they imagine they should be and to do what they think they should, both personally and professionally. In other words, they strive to achieve goals that originate out of an extrinsic motivation.

The real power to do what you can do, or be what you can be, however, originates from drivers deep inside your emotional brain. You tap into this powerful source of energy when your motives move from being externally to internally focused. 'Intrinsic motivation' emerges from a desire to engage in an activity because you value it for the inherent satisfaction it provides. Nothing builds your stocks of emotional capital more quickly.

When Michael Gerber, best-selling author of the E-Myth, was asked why what he does is so important to him, he replied:

> It was just there it showed up. And it was compelling. It was elegant. It took my breath away!...We have a purpose to create...creation is the act of producing something out of nothing, the love one finds in...it is enough to last a human being a lifetime.

This remarkable statement from one of the most successful businessmen on the planet reflects Gerber's passion. He sees no significant distinction between the intrinsic motivation to work, create, love and live. For Gerber, it's this intrinsic motivation, this 'passion of the soul and the passion of the mind', that produces vision and builds world-class businesses.

Strategy one — a passion for what you do

Yes, passion is at the heart of the emotional capitalist. Without passion, your stocks of emotional capital will quickly run dry and you will fall back on your technical skills in an attempt to drive your own productivity and the productivity of others.

Passion is powerful. It's the force that keeps you moving forwards and reaching for higher ground. It is the energy that fuels creativity, courage and compassion. Passion is a weird and wonderful thing. It's a life force that, in your best moments, energises and connects you to everything that really matters in your life. Conversely, its absence leaves you feeling disconnected, dependent and bored.

'All very well', I hear you saying, 'but what exactly is it?'

Satisfaction and pleasure

Passion lives somewhere between two very positive emotions — satisfaction and pleasure. In everyday English we do not often distinguish between these two similar emotions. A massage or a great bottle of red wine produces the positive emotions of pleasure; however, satisfaction points to something much deeper. Buddha suggested that the things that seem to lead to real satisfaction have something of an investment quality to them, such as building a house, creating a child or writing a book. Some people experience this feeling of satisfaction while painting a picture, leading a group, making music, making love or through a sporting endeavour. The experience is characterised by being totally absorbed in the flow of what's happening. What do we like about these experiences? The feeling of satisfaction and passion they produce.

Mihaly Csikszentmihalyi is a psychologist who interviewed thousands of people of all ages and asked them to describe their highest moments of satisfaction — an idea that he described in his book as 'flow'.[14] According to Mihaly, when people experience their highest satisfactions (flow), they often describe the psychological elements as, 'the task is challenging and requires skill', 'we concentrate', 'there are clear goals', 'we get immediate feedback', 'we have deep, effortless involvement', 'there is a sense of control', 'our sense of self vanishes' or 'time stops'.

Interestingly, none of these components are about the experience of pleasure per se. Rather, when we are absorbed in flow, it's about total engagement and a loss of self-consciousness. In other words, when we are wrapped up in flow we are investing in building emotional capital that we can draw on to sustain our passion and, therefore, our energy. In contrast to seeking the immediate rewards of a pleasurable experience, to build your emotional capital you need to pay attention to the elements of the flow experience that fuel your passion and produce your most rewarding, hard-won satisfactions.

This means in order to reach self-actualisation you must: ensure that your abilities match the high challenge of your situation and opportunity; establish clear goals of what you're trying to achieve; focus your attention regularly on becoming the leader you want to be; establish a sense of control and take charge of developing your leadership skills; create your future by developing an attitude of positive self-expectancy; learn something valuable from each experience; minimise your narcissistic need to be admired, which leads to self-consciousness; cultivate a genuine self-awareness that is open to receiving feedback.

'Okay, Martyn', I can hear you say, 'all good advice if I want to become a SNAG (sensitive new age guy/girl) — but what has it got to do with my business?'

Actually, Jack Welch in his latest book, *Winning*, outlines the business case for passion when he says:

> *People with passion care — really care in their bones — about colleagues, employees, and friends winning. They love to learn and grow, and they get a huge kick when the people around them do the same.*

Welch's view is backed up by solid research. Investigators at the University of Rochester's human motivation research group found, for example, that people whose motivations were intrinsic—defined as 'self-anchored'—exhibited more interest, excitement and confidence, as well as greater persistence, creativity and performance than a control group of subjects who were motivated largely by external demands and rewards.[15]

In other words, passionate people are productive, persistent, high performers. They look for creative challenges, love learning new things and take great pride in a job well done. They often seem bored with the status quo and display a constant energy for discovering how things can be improved.

Throughout my life, people have frequently asked me where I get my enthusiasm from. I used to reply, 'I don't honestly know, it's just there. It kind of rises up when something captures my imagination and I can see the possibility of creating something new'. These days, although I still don't fully understand where it comes from, I certainly know a lot more about how to get it and keep it. Certainly Mihaly's ideas on flow help us to understand a lot more about the components that are involved in generating and sustaining this passionate energy. Here are a few more discoveries to help build your emotional capital in this vital area.

Discovery 1 — the gift of creative discontent

Who looks at discontent as a gift?[16] Not many of us. But if you have spent your life seeing things the same old way, and it gets harder and harder to keep the fire in the belly, then it is time to tune in to your discontent, but creatively. Becoming aware of your discontent is the first positive step in fuelling your passion. It keeps you from settling for the status quo. By refusing to accept the way things are—by declining to say, 'you just can't do that', 'near enough is good enough', 'that'll never work' or 'just get on with things as they are' — you continually generate new ways of looking at things, creating vision. These statements are at the heart of your discontent and are potential catalysts for change.

Discovery 2 — where you stand determines what you see

'Where you stand determines what you see' is an obvious statement if ever there was one. Of course where we stand determines what we see — and where we stand is determined by a lot of things. Factors such as our upbringing, our education, or lack of it, the way we look, our degree of talent and our financial security all determine our point of view. However, none of these things matter in developing passion. Passion is born out of the creative discontent that happens when you compare your expectations of how things could be with the daily experience of how they are now. It all starts with a vision of what you can see. Never mind where you stand, what can you see? If you can't see anything really exciting, try standing somewhere else! Then, when your vision begins to develop, keep your mind focused on what you would like to achieve and you will intensify the feelings necessary to transform your thoughts into actions.

I was recently talking to Dustin Wilson, the head coach of the Chinese olympic aerial ski team. He's discovered that what the best skiers have in common is the ability to visualise the kind of performance they want to produce, even if the trick has never been attempted before. World-class aerial skiers use this visualisation technique to imagine the impossible. Mind you, it's not only sportspeople who have used the power of visualisation to their advantage. All world-class entrepreneurs were attempting the impossible at the beginning of their careers too.

By cultivating and enlarging your vision you fuel your passion.

Discovery 3 — who you listen to determines what you hear

It's obvious that who you listen to determines what you hear, but what is not so obvious is that we often make great efforts to associate with people who see the world the way we do, and avoid those who might challenge our view. In addition to the quality of your vision, which is born of discontent, the most influential factor in developing your passion will be the voices of other people in your life. If you want to build and sustain your passion, associate with other passionate people. Listen to them and learn from their experience. It's a psychological truth that you will become more and more like the people with whom you most identify. So, mix with the brightest and best, and if your social circle is a little short on entrepreneurs, at least get to the bookstore and read their stories to fuel your inspiration.

Discovery 4 — what you do determines who you are

This discovery's not so obvious. In fact, most of us think the opposite is true, that who we are determines what we do. But it doesn't really work that way, because it suggests that it's easy to make the leap from thought to action. For example, people say that their family is the most important priority in their lives and yet they choose to spend excessively long hours at work. We find it easy to say we believe in something, such as caring for the environment, yet we engage in actions that are the exact opposite — such as continuing with a lifestyle of excessive consumption of nonrenewable resources.

The opposite approach is more accurate. Who you really are is forged by your actions. Although your thoughts and feelings affect your behaviour, it's equally true that your behaviour affects your thoughts and feelings. In other words, what you do determines who you really are.

This truth is not all together new. Ancient Greek and Hebrew philosophers believed you could only really know something or someone through active experience. The well-known American philosopher and psychologist William James believed that it is easier to act your way into a new kind of thinking than it is to think yourself into a new way of acting. He described the 'act as if' principle as an effective strategy for changing the way we think and feel about ourselves. According to James, if you want a quality such as passion, you should 'act as if' you already have it. The impact that this will have in the outer world, in changing how other people see you and treat you, will, in turn, help you to think about yourself differently.

Discovery 5 — how you feel determines how well you do

How you feel inside yourself on a daily basis will have a significant impact on the quality of what you produce. If you're like most people, your thoughts and feelings tend to be drawn by the gravitational pull of negativity. You are probably only too well aware of what you're not good at and what needs fixing. Organisations spend millions on training programs designed to 'fix' people with performance problems by targeting their 'weaknesses'— an altogether wrong approach.

A couple of years ago I was speaking at a conference organised by the British Psychological Society. Martin Seligman was also speaking on a recent movement in psychology known as 'positive psychology'. Positive psychology focuses on fostering people's strengths, rather than being preoccupied with addressing their weaknesses. Seligman, in his book *Authentic Happiness*, tells the story of one of his students, Julian, who kept an exotic Amazonian lizard as a pet.[17] In the first weeks after getting the lizard the student could not get it to eat. He tried everything, but it continued to

WHO YOU REALLY ARE IS FORGED BY YOUR ACTIONS

starve. He offered it lettuce, then mango, meat, flies, fruit juice and even Chinese takeout.

One day Julian offered it a ham sandwich, and there was still no reaction. Going about his daily routine he picked up a newspaper and threw it down on top of the sandwich. The lizard took one look and crept stealthily across the floor, leapt onto the newspaper, shredded it, and then ate the sandwich. The lizard needed to stalk and shred before it would eat. Seligman's point is that lizard's have evolved to stalk and pounce and shred before they eat. Hunting is one of a lizard's strengths, and it is so essential that the lizard's appetite could not be awakened until it had been engaged.

Human beings are far more complex than lizards, but, according to Seligman, all of our complexity sits on top of an emotional brain designed to exercise our personal strengths. We cannot bypass it in the pursuit of immediate pleasure and still be at our best. Indeed, we are at our best when our personal strengths are engaged.

To increase your passion, focus your attention on your positive strengths. Value who you are, what you do and what you have. This is the most straightforward way to increase your feelings of wellbeing and happiness, and increase your passion. You'll feel better and, as a result, you will be more effective.

Everything's turned upside down

Maslow suggested that, traditionally, we all start at the bottom of the hierarchy of needs, satisfying our hunger and slowly moving towards self-actualisation. Today, things can get turned upside down. Financial reward is only one of many things that motivate people. Many people go for self-actualisation first — then the rest. They are prepared to forgo some of the basic needs for a while in order to travel to India, or to buy a mountain bike or a piece of original art.

You may remember, for example, that for generations education was based on humiliation, beatings, fail grades and even the dunce's cap. Then, more enlightened educators recognised that students produced their best work when rewarded for their strengths, or when coached to acquire specialist knowledge. In particular, we discovered that a teacher with a positive attitude could have a profound effect on students' performance — the 'Pygmalion effect' described in the next chapter. This all suggests that there is a more powerful route to increasing productivity in people than a simple cash reward.

At work, people are at their very best when they have the opportunity to maximise their skills and interests. The Gallup Organization found that the most satisfied workers affirmatively answered the question, 'Does your job allow you every day to do what you are truly best at?' Work that creates opportunities for people to shine results in greater flow experiences, which, in turn, is a direct investment leading to increased productivity.

When you, as a leader, appeal to people's signature strengths, you engage the primary drivers of human performance — values.

PEOPLE ARE AT THEIR VERY BEST WHEN THEY HAVE THE OPPORTUNITY TO MAXIMISE THEIR SKILLS AND INTERESTS

People want to work for leaders who hold values that are in accordance with their own. These days, people value a worthwhile mission and great working lifestyle as much as they do a cash incentive and the prospect of promotion. As a leader, if you give real meaning to people's work and the freedom and resources to pursue their ideas, then you will be a good boss to work for.

There are, undoubtedly, bad bosses, toxic work environments, difficult relationships and real life crises. Nonetheless, we have far more control over our energy than we ordinarily realise. The more people rely on external motivators — sticks and carrots — the more limited and compromised will be the energy they bring to work. The more people are able to engage their signature strengths and take responsibility for their work, the more empowered and productive they become. This lies at the heart of building real emotional capital, and it is critical for building high performance in business.

Strategy two — a work–life balance

The second aspect of self-actualisation involves establishing a work–life balance. You see, passion is all very well, but the problem with passionate people is that they're not only excited about work. As Jack Welch puts it, 'They tend to be passionate about everything'.

The challenge of great performance is to manage your emotional energy more effectively in all dimensions to achieve your goals. Too often we think in terms of conflicts — this versus that, or work versus life — instead of complements, as though the different responsibilities we have are at odds with each other. This is a certain recipe for emotional depletion.

Instead of being pushed and pulled by competing forces, you must create balance in your life that enables you to lead with greater flow.

How do you take control of your time and attention in today's pressured environment?

No-one has to tell you that you have many roles to play and many responsibilities to take into account. While perfect balance may be unrealistic, it certainly helps to develop a strong central platform from which to identify and coordinate all those competing demands.

The eight-fold path

Career specialist Laurence Boldt has described a model that is useful for taking back control.[18] Boldt suggests there are four essential dimensions to your experience: the practical you, the potential you, the productive you and the personal you. Each of the areas is complementary, with success in one area increasing opportunities for success in the others:

1 *The practical you*: according to Boldt, this involves that part of you that wants to manage your life. It recognises the primary importance of your physical health, not only for its own sake, but also for the role it plays in providing stability and energy necessary for achieving success in the other areas. It is also concerned with establishing a lifestyle that reflects the values that are most important to you.

2 *The potential you*: this includes that part of you that seeks to become your best. This area is all about self-development and creative expression. Whether through your vocation or recreation, your potential requires a vehicle to create something of value.

3 *The productive you*: Boldt suggests that this involves the part of you that wants to achieve a meaningful life's work, to share your unique abilities, and to make a difference in the lives of others. It's the aspect of you that wants a rewarding and challenging career and is also concerned with achieving financial success.

4 *The personal you*: this part of you wants to relate to others and seeks a rich and rewarding social life. It's the part of you that wants to feel a sense of belonging and community. It is also the aspect of you that is concerned with your intimate relationships, including the need for companionship, stimulating sex and a rewarding family life.

Investment in all of these dimensions builds your overall stocks of emotional capital. The challenge of great performance as a leader is coordinating capital in all these areas to achieve your goals. All four dimensions are critical, none is sufficient by itself, and each profoundly influences the others.

To perform at your best you must skillfully manage each of these interconnected dimensions of energy. The responsibilities of leadership often involve taking up challenges that push you beyond your ordinary limits, creating stress and placing demands on you. Any form of stress that puts you under pressure has the potential to build your emotional capacity. Just as physical energy is spent and renewed, so too is emotional energy. To be productive as a leader you must know how to fully engage in a challenge, but also how to disengage and renew resources. Like any capitalist system, wealth is created by a careful balance of investing and spending — and building emotional capital is no different.

STRESS THAT PUTS YOU UNDER PRESSURE HAS THE POTENTIAL TO BUILD YOUR EMOTIONAL CAPACITY

You are a living 'open system'. You constantly interact with your environment and change it. You have the capacity to create chaos or harmony, to be self-destructive or create wellness and fulfillment. You can choose to eat to excess, drive too fast, work too hard and lose control of your emotions. Or you can eat properly, drive carefully, balance your work with recreation and take control of your emotional life.

Habits of the heart

If you're like me, the chances are you've been told 'it's all about being more disciplined'. Personally, I've never been a big believer in discipline. Discipline is really a push strategy. Instead, I'm convinced that the things we do best we do because we are compelled to do them, and that we do them almost on automatic pilot. It's a pull strategy. Sure, strong will and discipline push us to excel, but real performance is achieved when we're pulled forward by the things we really want to do. Take, for example, something as simple as brushing your teeth. It is not something that you ordinarily have to remind yourself to do. Brushing your teeth is something to which you feel drawn consistently, compelled by its clear health value.

However, there is a second issue to be addressed here — habit. You brush your teeth largely on automatic pilot without much conscious effort or attention. Compare this with flossing your teeth. It has the same health value as brushing your teeth, but, for some, it simply hasn't become a daily habit because

REAL PERFORMANCE IS ACHIEVED WHEN WE'RE PULLED FORWARD BY THE THINGS WE REALLY WANT TO DO

it is something you learn in childhood. But for those who didn't learn that habit, flossing their teeth every day is a chore. They know that they must floss to prevent gum disease, but they have trouble remembering to do it. If you tell people that you floss every day they are amazed and may remark how disciplined you must be. In fact, it's not about discipline at all. After all, you know the things you would accomplish if only you had more discipline, right?

Every day we act with discipline, except it doesn't feel like discipline because our actions have become unconscious habits.

In other words, you achieve best practice when two forces combine — when your values are engaged and when you practise emotionally intelligent behaviours until they become habitual. The power of these habits, when balanced with your values, is that they require little conscious energy, leaving you free to focus your emotional capital on strategic objectives that create wealth in the fullest sense of the word. After all, it was Aristotle who said, 'We are what we repeatedly do. Excellence, then, is not an act, but a habit'.

Summary

Developing self-actualisation as an emotional competency is the real source of power behind sustained high performance. The skillful development and management of your emotional energy will ultimately determine the quality of your productivity at work and in life generally. The passion that is at the heart of the emotional capitalist has little to do with determination, commitment, or even with obtaining what you think is missing from your life. It is an intrinsic motivation that arises from somewhere deep within. Passion is an emotional competency you can develop by focusing your attention on your discontent — what you are unhappy with or what you'd like to do better — and then cultivating a vision of how things could be different. Furthermore, your passion is increased by listening to other passionate voices and then acting as if the change you wish to see has already occurred. Finally, by continually valuing your signature strengths you will harness the power of this creative energy and enable it to work productively for you.

You should make every effort to ensure that people are given opportunities to shine at what they do, therefore increasing the possibility of greater flow experiences at work. This means people should be given tasks that present creative challenges, have clear goals and provide people with a sense of control and positive self-expectancy. Finally, you must give positive feedback.

To maximise your emotional capital you should aim to create balance in your life by ensuring that all the important areas of your life get the attention they deserve. This means regularly paying attention to the interconnected dimensions of the eight-fold path until these practices become habits of the heart.

The process of self-actualisation is about becoming all that you can be and doing all that you can do. It will enable others to believe they can do the same. This is leadership.

Building emotional capital

Strategies for developing self-actualisation

☑ Do 'what you can' — make a decision to take up the pen and author you own experience from here on.

☑ Pay attention to the elements of the flow experience that fuel your passion.

☑ Establish clear goals of what you're trying to achieve; regularly focus your attention on becoming the leader you want to be.

☑ Cultivate a genuine self-awareness that is open to receiving feedback.

☑ Become aware of your discontent — identify what you are unhappy with, what you want to do better, and what you would like to change.

☑ Cultivate and enlarge your vision to fuel your passion.

☑ Mix it with the brightest and best, and read the stories of successful leaders to fuel your inspiration.

☑ Act 'as if' you already are the leader you imagine yourself being.

☑ Focus your attention on your positive strengths, value who you are, what you do and what you have.

☑ Appeal to people's signature strengths and provide people with opportunities to shine by giving tasks that:
   - present creative challenges
   - have clear goals
   - provide a sense of control and positive self-expectancy.

☑ Give positive feedback regularly.

☑ Ensure that all the eight important areas of your life get the regular attention they deserve.

Nothing splendid has ever been achieved except by those who dared believe that something inside them was superior to circumstance.

Bruce Barton

Self-esteem is the reputation we acquire with ourselves.

Nathaniel Branden

6 Self-confidence

Another consistently high score in the studies that differentiate high-performing leaders from others was obtained for self-confidence. How you view yourself crucially affects virtually every aspect of your experience. Certainly, feeling good about yourself is a solid defence against emotional difficulties, but unless it's built on a platform of sound achievement it can remain, at best, unconvincing and, at worst, arrogant self-absorption. In other words, self-confidence is built on two pillars: a feeling of personal worth and a feeling of personal competence. Solid self-confidence is important because it is the platform that supports your ability to respond actively and positively to value-creating opportunities. It is also the most basic foundation of your emotional capital and the source of your personal power.

Self-confidence is the emotional component of your personality and the most important factor in determining how you think, feel and behave. Your level of self-confidence largely determines what you make happen in life. The higher your self-confidence — the more you like and respect yourself — the more you will like and respect others and the better they will feel towards you. In your business, your personal level of self-confidence will be the critical factor determining whether or not people will buy from you, employ you, perform for you and enter into business dealings with you.

Mirror, mirror on the wall

People have been talking to 'mirrors' throughout history. Just about everything you know or believe about yourself has been conditioned by the mirror of people's reactions to you. Many of these reactions have comprised critical statements about you not being up to it, or about you being inadequate in one way or another. They are often associated with social or working conditions that make your worth dependent on performing certain behaviours. When you fail to perform to the satisfaction of others you internalise their disapproval, and this contributes another pixel to the picture of your self-confidence. Of course, more positive expressions of your personal worth and value contribute to you developing a more likable image of yourself. Similarly, the feedback you receive about how well you deal with certain challenges determines, to a large extent, how confident you feel about your abilities.

Taken all together, these images of yourself are linked to emotional experiences and recorded on the hard drive of your personality, determining your level of self-confidence.

The good, the bad and the ugly

Overall, your self-confidence is a collection of all the images and beliefs about yourself and your abilities. Whether you see yourself as the good, the bad or the ugly, is the result of a collection of beliefs spawned from the experiences, choices, achievements, failures, ideas, emotions and opinions in your life to date. For example, imagine you're about to make an important presentation to a new client. Suddenly, you find yourself remembering the time in sixth grade when you stood up in front of the school to speak at your graduation and your mind went blank and you had nothing to say. You become self-conscious and anxious at the very thought of making this presentation. Often, these experiences, along with the messages we pick up from other people, become unconscious stories that define the way we view ourselves — these stories contribute to our self-confidence.

Who is screening your calls

If you grew up in an environment in which you were continually criticised, you probably learned to focus on your faults and inadequacies. You may do a number of things really well, but when you make a simple mistake you enlarge it out of proportion. It's like your attention is conditioned to ignore the things you have done well; instead it is drawn like a magnet to focus on the negative parts of your performance. And there is a direct relationship between your performance in any area and your level of self-confidence. Your level of self-confidence acts like a personal assistant (PA) filtering the information to only bring to your attention the values that are consistent with your view of yourself. In other words, your self-confidence — your PA — influences the way you screen your incoming calls.

Imagine that you have just completed a difficult assignment at work. Your performance was outstanding and your colleagues have told you so. A 'call' informing your awareness of this success is received. The PA screening the calls says, 'I'm sorry, he or she is not available'. Later in the day, you make an embarrassing mistake in front of a client that you are trying to impress.

On this occasion, the call comes in and your PA says, 'Thanks for calling, I'll connect you straightaway'. It's as though your PA has been given a script of the criteria by which to screen the incoming calls. Your script directs your PA to focus on data that supports the image you have of yourself as incompetent or unlikable.[19]

Your self-confidence establishes a benchmark against which you can evaluate your performance and determine how well you think you are doing. In other words, your self-confidence acts like an internal mirror and ensures that performance on the outside is consistent with the image held on the inside. This lies at the core of your personality and has a dramatic impact on how you perform as a leader.

The twin towers

More practically, self-confidence is built on the twin emotions of self-liking — liking and accepting who you are — and self-competence — a feeling of being on top of a situation and possessing the resources and skills to manage life's challenges.[20] High levels of these emotions allow you to feel good about yourself, sustain high levels of motivation and maintain positive and productive relationships with others. The more you like and respect yourself and the more self-confidence you have in your capacity to perform various tasks, the more likely you are to possess the motivation and drive to achieve your goals.

Strategy one — self-liking

The first of the twin towers of self-confidence — self-liking — is best defined as your level of self-esteem. The more you like yourself, the better you perform at anything you attempt.

Your reactor core

Your self-esteem is the 'reactor core' of your personality. It is the energy source that determines your levels of confidence and enthusiasm. The more you like yourself, the higher the standards you set for yourself. The more you like yourself, the bigger your goals and the longer you will persist in achieving them.

How much you like yourself is largely determined by how closely your self-image and current performance and behaviour match your self-ideal — your picture of how you would perform if you were at your very best. Your self-ideal is the person you would most like to become. It is made up of all the virtues, values and qualities that you most admire in yourself and others. These ideas guide and shape your behaviour. Very clear about their values, visions and ideals, great leaders know who they are and what they believe in. They set high standards for themselves, and they don't compromise those standards. They are people that others can look up to and depend on.

GREAT LEADERS ARE VERY CLEAR ABOUT THEIR VALUES, VISIONS AND IDEALS

I'm okay — you're okay

Over 30 years ago Thomas Harris wrote a book with a catchy title that became an overnight bestseller, *I'm Ok — You're Ok*.[21] Harris suggested that by virtue of their inferior power in an adult world, children make an unconscious decision and learn that 'I'm not okay', and that being an adult is 'okay'.

But there's good news. Once you are aware that it was a decision you made as a child, largely automatically, you can decide to replace it with a relaxed, self-liking mode of being. This, however, doesn't happen automatically. Each adult has to make a conscious decision to totally accept themselves as they are. This requires that you shift authority from an external locus of control, in which you make decisions based on what other people want, to an internal locus of control in which you make decisions based on your values and beliefs. Although you may not be everything you would ideally like to be, the most important decision you will ever make is that you are 'okay' — in fact, better than okay, actually likable.

Once you make this decision you can stop trying to prove yourself and instead begin expressing yourself. From here you are better able to establish an internal dialogue reminding you that although you're not everything you are going to be, thankfully, you're not what you were.

Perhaps no obstacle to high performance is as pervasive and difficult as lack of confidence and low self-confidence.

When I met Julie T, she was the producer of a successful movie distribution business, but, like many people, lived with the constant worry that one day she would be exposed as the impostor she thought she was. She was convinced that if people really knew her they wouldn't like her. As a result, she was cautious about getting too close to her colleagues and kept all her interactions cool and businesslike. She would rarely disclose what she really thought, much less what she really felt, particularly with clients who may have strong views of their own and question her judgement. On her good days she would take strong positions and find herself almost belligerent and uncompromising; on bad days she would simply acquiesce and comply with decisions to avoid conflict that may expose her ignorance or uncertainty. Consequently, she found it hard to be authentic, people around her were losing confidence in her leadership, and clients were beginning to doubt her competence to manage their products.

I began by helping Julie to change her focus from worrying about how others viewed her, to concentrating on being guided by her own views and values. I suggested that, even though she may not be everything that she would like to be as a person, she needed to make a fundamental decision to accept the person she was. We then discussed the values that were most fundamental to her. It turned out that she identified honesty and respect as the two most important, neither of which she demonstrated in her work relationships. It was not that she would deliberately deceive or mislead people, she simply wouldn't tell people what she really thought for fear they may disagree and reject her.

As Julie began to identify the values that defined her as a person, she increasingly began to measure herself by her own internal standards. She realised that she had earned the right to her views and that they really were an expression of her values. By accepting herself and establishing clearer boundaries around herself and the views that belonged to her, she was able to allow others the freedom to do the same, even if it meant disagreeing with them.

Julie discovered that as she became less concerned about how other people viewed her, she was able to lead from the front more often. She was also surprised to discover that she felt more comfortable with being consultative in her approach with her colleagues and wasn't so afraid that they would think her ignorant.

In fact, I reminded her that, actually, everybody's ignorant, just on different subjects!

By not working so hard to be the expert all the time she found a genuine reciprocity developing in her relationships, and her clients appreciated her transparency and clarity.

I'm okay, but…

Just pause for a moment and reflect on the idea that you're okay the way you are. Before long, the chances are that your next thought includes a large 'but', such as, 'I'm okay the way I am, but I should be better at ...' or 'I'm okay, but I wish I was more ...' These automatic thoughts indicate that in some way or other you're attacking yourself.

Now, there's nothing wrong with aspiring to improve yourself as a person, but self-acceptance is the ability to accept yourself in the moment, with compassion and without judgement.

Gratitude and generosity

The first step towards self-acceptance is learning to recognise and accept your feelings. Feelings are the most accurate way of understanding your emotional needs. The next step involves suspending judgement of yourself and letting go of the idea that you need other people to approve of you to feel accepted. The next critical step is to recognise that all that you are and all that you have is a gift. You didn't do anything to deserve what you have or who you are. Instead, be generous to yourself and develop an attitude of gratitude for your experience and value and respect your distinctive qualities and the person that you've become. In this way you can allow the person you are becoming to expand and change, while celebrating yourself as a person.

Strategy two — self-competence

The second tower that supports your self-confidence is your self-competence — how you evaluate yourself as competent.

Your inner mirror

Your self-competence is often called your 'inner mirror'. It's where you look internally to evaluate your performance in a particular situation.

Because of the power of your self-image, on the outside you always consistently act with the picture you have of yourself on the inside. Again, this picture is largely the result of the things you have heard repeated about yourself. Heinz Kohut, a world authority on self psychology, tells the story of how children develop self-competence. Imagine a child who is faced with the opportunity to climb a tall tree. Inspired by a growing sense of confidence in his or her big idea, the child decides to climb to the top. One parent, on discovering his child at the top of the tree, yells out, 'What are you doing up there? Get down at once and don't let me ever see you do such a thing again!' The child descends immediately and makes an automatic decision to place less trust in that big idea next time around — opting instead to become more conventional.

On the other hand, another parent responds differently. Instead of rebuking his child, he or she chooses to encourage such independence with a comment such as, 'Wow! How did you manage to get up there by yourself? You must be able to see forever, well done. Next time, though, let me know, so I can make sure you're safe'. The message conveyed is very different and the child has the opportunity to cement another brick in the wall of his or her sense of personal competence.

Self-talk

In a study conducted by a leading American university, graduate students followed two-year-old children around and recorded every time their parents said something positive to them and every time they said something negative. The results were startling. On average, the children heard 432 negative and 32 positive statements per day, a ratio of 14 to one. Over the course of your development, these, and thousands of messages like them, form the raw material you use to automatically construct your sense of personal competence.

Negative beliefs gained in early years are carried over into later life. In another study, conducted at the University of California, Los Angeles, first-year students were asked to list their personal strengths and weaknesses. They were bright students, yet their lists of weaknesses were six times longer than their lists of strengths!

Throughout the day you are constantly talking to yourself. Psychologists estimate that we hear up to 500 words a minute in our 'mind's ear'. That's a lot of talk. What you heard repeated over and over as a child, you came to believe as fact. Once your subconscious mind accepts a belief through repeated hearings, it, in turn, begins to repeat that belief inside your head. Do you find yourself saying things to yourself like, 'there's something wrong with me', 'people like me can't do that', 'it's all my fault', 'nothing I ever do turns out right'? We all practise self-talk. Some of our internal self-talk is positive, but very often it is negative. This type of inner dialogue is called the 'inner critic' and it tends to collaborate with the PA I discussed earlier. The inner critic is constantly occupied with negative and critical thoughts about your competency, or, rather, a lack thereof. Negative self-talk is the most powerful trigger of anxiety, and it dramatically lowers your stocks of emotional capital, therefore limiting your performance as a leader.

SOME OF OUR INTERNAL SELF-TALK IS POSITIVE, BUT VERY OFTEN IT IS NEGATIVE

Twisted thinking

Psychologists determine that, in reality, the vast majority of negative self-talk causing so much emotional distress and performance dysfunction is actually filled with gross distortions. These distortions shape your judgements of your ability to cope with the circumstances, challenges and people you encounter in your daily life.

Psychologist Aaron Beck was one of the first psychologists to develop a set of categories to describe this type of dysfunctional thinking. His work has been popularised by David Burns, who called it 'twisted thinking'.

Twisted thinking can involve 'black or white thinking', where we look at things in absolutes or extremes and fail to notice the grey areas; 'jumping to conclusions', where we instantly reach a judgement without pausing to ensure we have all the necessary, reliable information; 'labelling', where we make negative value judgements about ourselves and criticise every imperfection; 'negative expectations', which is a form of pessimism explored in chapter 4 in our discussion of optimism; and, finally, 'overgeneralisation', where we take one experience and tell ourselves that every similar situation will have the same negative result.

Beck suggests that, as these thoughts were programmed into us as children, we can reprogram ourselves as adults to choose the way we think and, therefore, the way we feel and behave. He recommends that we recognise when we are having a negative thought, making a note of the situation and the feelings we experience. We can then use our reason to identify the ways in which the thought is actually distorted, and then reframe our perception to be more objective and positive.

Although more easily said than done, it actually works!

Over time you will actually shift the automatic assumptions that determine how you see situations and find new, more powerful feelings of competency in managing them.

'Okay', I hear you say, 'these are all very useful strategies for building my self-confidence, but what's it got to do with improving my leadership?'

How to win friends and influence people

Well, what's true for you is also true for people who work with you. If, in order to function at optimal levels, you need to feel liked and competent, so will the people who work for you. The more you tell people that you like them and what they need to do to be more competent, the easier it will be for you to set up a constructive relationship. Over the course of time, when people know you really like them and that you believe they are competent, they'll work well for you.

BEING ABLE TO BRING OUT THE BEST IN PEOPLE IS LARGELY BASED ON THE EXPECTATIONS YOU HAVE OF THEM

Because successful people deliver results, emotional capitalists look for ways to extend the psychological benefits of emotional wealth by helping their people feel successful.

Leaders who have sufficient emotional resources to overcome their egos make other people feel strong. They empower others to own the group's success by building their people's competence and by listening to their views.

Clearly, before we can lead we have to believe in ourselves and others. If you like yourself, not only will you be more effective and productive, but so will the people who work with you. Strong leaders bring out the best in people.

The Pygmalion effect

Being able to bring out the best in people is largely based on the expectations you have of them. Leaders who treat people in a way that supports their self-confidence make it possible for people to achieve things they initially thought impossible.

There is a well-documented method for increasing performance that consists of creating positive expectations of people — psychologists refer to it as the 'Pygmalion effect'. This phenomenon is based on the Greek myth about Pygmalion, a sculptor who carved a statue of a beautiful woman, then fell in love with it and brought it to life by the strength of his belief and desire. Research on the phenomenon of self-fulfilling prophecies provides plenty of evidence that people act in ways that are consistent with other people's expectations of them.

In his book *Pygmalion in the Classroom*, Robert Rosenthal, of Harvard University, describes how the expectations of teachers have a dramatic impact on the performance of their students. In a well-known experiment, three teachers at the start of a school year were commended by their principal for their outstanding performance the previous year. In recognition of their achievement they were told that each of them would be put in charge of a class of the highest achieving students, who were selected on the basis of IQ, and that they were expected to make solid academic gains of around 20 to 30 per cent in the coming year. In reality, the students had been chosen at random from their year level.

The classes were observed for the entire school year. At the end of the year, students in the three classes had achieved a gain of 20 to 30 per cent in academic achievement over the previous year. Naturally, the teachers were surprised, but explained the results as being evidence of their expertise as teachers. Imagine their surprise when they were told that they, too, had been chosen at random from the teaching staff and not on the basis of outstanding ability! This is what psychologists call a double-blind experiment — neither the students nor the teachers were aware of the experimental conditions. The only difference between these three classes and the rest of the school were the expectations the teachers had of themselves and their students.

Great expectations

The expectations you have of your people will have a dramatic impact on their performance. When you are a leader, people become what you tell them they are. If you communicate to the people who work for you how you want them to be, then you will increase the chance that they will meet your expectations. If you expect them to fail, you will increase the chance that they will. Likewise, if you expect them to succeed, you will greatly increase the chances that they will. Dealing with people respectfully, and in a friendly and positive way, communicates that you like them, are confident in their capacity to perform and that you value their contribution. This will greatly increase the likelihood of enhanced performance.

An important strategy for promoting positive expectations is to encourage people to set their own development goals. Similarly, instead of being the fount of all wisdom, create space for people to generate their own innovative solutions to business challenges.

Equally, when you have high expectations of yourself and realise the value of being an emotional capitalist, you will tend to provide your people with more support, give more feedback about the results of their efforts and be more open to their views. Once you get inside the emotional world of someone, he or she will be much more receptive to what you have to say. When you provide positive messages, it changes the way people perceive you and their reactions to you. This, in turn, changes the way you perceive yourself and has a positive impact on your personal self-confidence.

Summary

Building your self-confidence is the starting point for unlocking your potential and accomplishing more than you ever have before. If you want to change your performance and results in any area of your life, begin with improving your self-concept — your beliefs about yourself. It is vital for you to decide that, although you are not exactly how you would like to be, or everything you have the potential to be, nevertheless, you are okay. Of course, deciding that you're okay involves an honest appreciation of your competencies and the decision to focus on them and celebrate your achievements. This involves the decision to like yourself for who you are. Look into your inner mirror with honesty and clarity, and challenge the distorted images generated by fear, harsh judgements and criticism. Determine to like the core of who you are — and have the humility to realise that there's room for improvement. This entails making a commitment to become all that you can be by bringing out your best. Remember, too, that leaders often become a mirror for their people. Strong leaders provide reflections to their team of what success looks like and make sure individual contributions are celebrated.

Leaders don't often ask how they can create self-confidence in the workplace. But they do ask questions such as, 'what can I do to stimulate innovation and creativity?', 'what can I do to create loyal, hard-working employees?', and 'what can I do to stimulate greater levels of productivity?'. The questions are different, but the answer is the same — build self-confidence.

Building emotional capital

Strategies for developing self-confidence

☑ Make a conscious decision that you are okay, and totally accept yourself just as you are.

☑ Celebrate your achievements and remind yourself that although you're not everything you are going to be, thankfully, you're not what you were.

☑ Practise self-responsibility for your choices and actions, increase self-reliance and take control to achieve what you want.

☑ Practise self-assertion and communicate in an honest, straightforward way.

☑ Find ways each day to communicate to your people that you like them and feel that they are competent.

☑ Become a Pygmalion-like leader and let your people know that you expect them to succeed.

☑ Provide your team with support, give constant positive feedback about the results of their efforts, and be open to their views.

☑ Provide your people with challenging assignments that draw out their talent.

☑ Recognise and acknowledge those around you for their individual talents.

☑ Provide constructive feedback on how to improve performance.

Before you are a leader, success is all about growing yourself. When you become a leader, success is all about growing others.

Jack Welch

Tell me and I'll forget; show me and I may remember; involve me and I'll understand.

Chinese proverb

7 Relationship skills

How do male leaders differ from female leaders? It is perhaps one of the most frequent questions that I get asked when talking about leadership and EQ in the corporate setting. The research studies that we conducted found no overall difference in EQ between genders; however, the studies did uncover a few differences in specific EQ competencies. One of the biggest gender differences was found in scores on relationship skills. It may not surprise you to discover that women scored higher in this competency than men, suggesting that they are better at initiating, developing and maintaining relationships.

Relationship skills represent one of the most important emotional competencies characterising high-performing leaders. Building relationship skills as a business strategy, however, provides one of the biggest development challenges for many leaders. This is not about simply being 'Mr Nice Guy'.

It's about consciously managing and developing the most valuable asset a company or person possesses. Relationships represent a unique strategic resource. In today's competitive environment they often signify the only real competitive advantage for many businesses.

Because each of your business relationships is important in making your company successful, the real power of building emotional capital involves building relationship skills — not only with employees and customers, but also with everyone your business touches.

In other words, when I talk about relationships, it encompasses all the relations that your organisation has with every group or individual that it comes into contact with. Relationships within your organisation, and also those with groups and individuals outside the business, form what I call the *relationship network*.

Some business strategists suggest that it's best to think of all these people as stakeholders — as people with a stake in the success of the organisation. I prefer to think of them as partners. In day-to-day practice, strong business partnerships are built on solid personal relationships. Because relationships are personal, leaders must make sure that they take responsibility for their relationship networks. Strong leaders consciously manage relationships at various levels among all partners — including those within the organisation.

Strategic partnerships

Business relationships thrive when each relationship is treated as a partnership. This approach can be contrasted with more traditional relationship models that are more transactional, paternal or adversarial.[22]

In traditional transactional relationships, employees are treated as commodities that have a set price and are owed nothing but that price. People are valued only because of the tasks they must perform. The relationship has a 'What have you done for me today?' feel to it.

Alternatively, leaders can establish more paternal relationships. This approach is similar to the relationship between caring parents and their children. Paternalistic leaders and organisations provide security and additional benefits, but the goal is to control. People are not encouraged to exercise independent judgement and most decisions go to the boss for approval.

Far worse are adversarial relationships, which are characterised by mistrust, tension and conflict. In many cases the conflict isn't always externalised, but exists, instead, in a passive-aggressive form. In these circumstances, people don't always have the courage to voice their discontent; however, their behaviour of resistance, begrudging compliance and a lack of initiative will act as a subtle saboteur of your best efforts. The underlying assumption in this model is that each person in the relationship is only looking out for themself, and withholding value from the other person in order to achieve his or her own ends — resulting in a 'win–lose' situation.

Partnership is fundamentally different to these three models. It emphasises a collaborative approach and a willingness to distribute power so that everyone can contribute and win — a 'win–win situation'. If partnership is the fundamental commitment required, then relationship skills are the strategic practice.

Egalité, mutualité, and liberté — vive la révolution!

As a strategy, relationship skills involve establishing three conditions. First, that relationships work best when people are recognised and treated as equals. It's the same for all of us — none of us like to be thought of as inferior or subordinate. Seeing people as similar to you, and therefore your equal, sets up a collaborative relationship. Even though partners in the relationship may be at different levels in the organisation, you must conduct each and every interaction as if both partners are equals. The fact is, both partners need each other to achieve mutual wins anyway.

PEOPLE WORK BEST WHEN THEY OWN THE RELATIONSHIP BY HAVING THE FREEDOM TO CONTRIBUTE TO IT

This notion of winning leads us to the second condition. People don't collaborate with you just because they like you. They will work well for you, and with you, when you are able to provide wins — benefits for them. In other words, it's a condition founded on recognising what other people need and want, and then aiming to create mutual wins for all partners in the relationship.

Third, effective relationships possess an element of autonomy. People in relationships are stakeholders and people work best when they own the relationship by having the freedom to contribute to it. This means that relationship skills based on partnerships involve the conscious decision to distribute power among all individuals with a stake in the business.

Engaging with people as partners enables you to adopt an approach that rewards wins, positive interactions and sustainable relationships.

No business, whatever the size, can function without collaborative relationships, because they provide the context in which people do business. When that context is missing — when people don't really know one another, or when relationships are distorted by mistrust or bad feelings — doing business becomes far more difficult. Your key challenge, as a leader committed to becoming an emotional capitalist, is to engage the hearts and minds, and emotions and intellects of your people to deliver superior service and business performance. Establishing, building, and maintaining well-planned and managed relationships is fundamental to the success of your business.

Equality, mutual wins and freedom for all — long live the revolution!

Strategy one — treat people as equals

Business brings you into contact with a wide range of people. To establish effective connections with these people you must be able to relate to them. Regardless of your status in the organisation, you wouldn't think of treating people differently based on their race or sex, would you? Similarly, if you judge others based on their role, place in the organisation or technical specialty, you'll find it harder to connect with them. Those differences are based on ancient ideas of political hierarchy that emphasised differences rather than similarities. Effective interpersonal connections happen when you focus on commonalities rather than differences.

Greek philosopher Dionysius introduced the concept of hierarchy over 1500 years ago.[23] The word literally means 'to rule through the sacred'. Dionysius was also interested in heaven and hell. He argued that heaven was hierarchically organised into exactly nine levels. In this model, God would be the CEO, the archangels would make up the top management team, and Jesus Christ would be in a staff position to the right of God. Dionysius also argued that hell had a similar organisational hierarchy, but with the pyramid turned upside down.

According to management theorists Jonas Ridderstråle and Kjell Nordström, in their book *Funky Business*, hierarchy builds on three key assumptions: a stable environment, predictable processes and output. In other words you know where you are, what you do and what will happen — the same competitors, customers, suppliers, technologies and product offerings year in and year out.[24] The chances are that this traditional model does not characterise your reality — and neither should it characterise the way you approach people connected with your business.

Sticks and carrots versus values and vibes

The traditional hierarchy has been turned on its head. Nowadays, people with relevant information are challenging traditional types of authority. When dealing with generation X and Y, remember that power now belongs to the people. In the traditional model, intimidation and threats were the established means for motivating performance. While command and control still remain influential, when power is in the hands of the people appeals to authority are less convincing — especially for people who may no longer be so obedient.

In fact, the Gallup Organisation found that no single factor predicts the productivity of an employee more clearly than his or her relationship with a direct supervisor. More specifically, Gallup found that the key drivers of productivity for employees are feeling cared for by a supervisor or someone at work, receiving recognition or praise in the past seven days and regular encouragement of development.

It's an obvious point, and one that I made in chapter 5, but it bears repeating: the drivers of performance are not sticks (rules) and carrots (rewards)! No — they are values and vibes. The things that really matter to people are having respect and trust, and feeling valued and having the opportunity to contribute value. The same principles can be applied to all relationships — in and around the business.

The way you approach your partners largely determines how they respond to you. Generally, your inner feelings about people determine your approach. Therefore, you must strengthen the belief that people are basically your equals and interact with them on equal terms.

Strategy two — create wins for everybody

Business consultants Tom Richardson, Augusto Vidaurreta and Tom Gorman suggest that virtually every person you want to do business with is similar to you in that they want wins of some kind. Find out what those wins are and what role you can play in creating them, and you're on the way to a collaborative relationship.[25]

You may remember that in chapter 3 I talked about emotional contracts — the unwritten set of expectations, needs and assumptions that holds people in relationships with others, including the organisation. Well, the single most important need in an emotional contract is, consciously or unconsciously, 'What's in it for me?'

This is particularly true of the current generation of young professionals, who were brought up, more often than not, not knowing the difficulties and deprivations of their parents' generation. Also, you may remember that in chapter 5, about Maslow's heirarchy of needs, I suggested that, today, many people's pyramid of needs have been turned upside down. Sure, pay is still important, but according to management guru Frederick Hertzberg, it's a 'hygiene factor' that people only notice when it's not up to standard. In fact, after more than a decade of studying what internal customers say they want, Kevin Thomson identified people's top ten personal needs as: great recruitment; great induction programs; a great boss and leadership; great training and development; great future and security; great career opportunities in and around the organisation; involvement in change; appropriate reward and recognition; great quality of work and work environment; and good communication that allows people to have an influence.[26]

It isn't any wonder that leadership fails when it focuses on transactional, paternal or adversarial approaches. Look at the top ten personal needs. Why would you want to perform at your best when you don't feel leadership is genuinely interested in you as a person? As Thomson puts it, 'Where is the what's in it for me?'

Increasing the trust quotient

Creating a context that focuses on mutual interest increases the trust quotient. By approaching others in a trusting manner, with a willingness to enter only win–win relationships, you will earn their trust. They will see you taking steps to gain their trust and they will respect you for it. When you focus on treating others as equals, you establish a collaborative foundation of, 'I don't win unless you win, and you don't win unless I win'. That's why you can even begin a discussion with, 'If we work together, here are ways I think I can win and ways I think you can win. What do you think?'

Wins need not always be spectacular. Many people see wins in being able to develop new skills, celebrate team accomplishments or in having better career prospects. However, one thing is certain — everybody wants to work well for, and feel good about, the boss. When an employee feels this way it's a win for him or her and for you.

Think of it this way: rather than seeking to establish control, try taking a trusting approach. Approach your people with an attitude that suggests 'I'm on good terms with this person and I trust them'. This is

MOST PEOPLE'S NEGATIVE BEHAVIOUR IS A PROTECTIVE DEVICE

the key to gaining and maintaining partnerships. When you are seeking the support of others, you are asking them to trust your ideas, your mission and your products or services. Most of all, you are asking them to trust you. The less people trust you, the greater their resistance, and the more energy expended to win their confidence and motivate them to move with you towards your goals. As you'll discover in the next chapter, trusting relationships are built on shared experiences as well as shared differences.

Knowing some personal details about the people with whom you're building a partnership enables you to understand what you have in common and how your experiences differ. This kind of personal information allows you to understand which types of wins really mean something to people.

'Okay', I hear you saying, 'this goes beyond my job description!'

Of course, I'm not suggesting here that you must experience life-changing events together, share intimate confidences or even deeply personal information. But to know each other as people, you must exchange some level of personal information and move beyond talking only about business and knowing one another only in terms of your business roles.

'But what if I don't like the son of a bitch?'

Sure, there are people who rub us up the wrong way, and people who are downright toxic, but if they're associated with the success of your business, you've got to find some humanity in them and find something to like. I'm a big believer in most people's negative behaviour being a protective device. People are usually afraid of losing things, such as control, esteem and status. By finding something in them that you like, and focusing on that strength whenever you do business with them, you create the potential for a trusting relationship. In the process, you may also encourage them to emerge from their protective shell and discover their humanity.

Okay, okay, so you're not the Dalai Lama. But you'd be surprised by how often controlling and intimidatory people actually change their approach over time when they encounter people who consistently respond to them with integrity. Bon courage!

To build emotional capital in your business you need to demonstrate that you are committed to meeting the needs of all partners. When people start to feel good about themselves, their organisation and their leaders, customers enjoy doing business with you. Your stocks of emotional capital rise dramatically and people buy-in to your initiatives. The win for you is that people want to be involved in what you're trying to achieve—they want to be part of the action and contribute in some way to making a difference.

This brings us to the third condition for building successful relationship skills.

Strategy three — provide autonomy

One of the most important psychological wins that partners in a relationship need is the ability to choose. It is the third element of effective relationship skills. Choice builds our sense of power and control over our lives — our autonomy.

The power of choice

As a leader, if you want higher levels of performance and greater initiative from your people, then you must be proactive in designing work that allows people discretion and choice. In other words, you must empower them.

I recently had a conversation with a senior manager of a large multinational beverage organisation and I asked him, 'What sort of a leader are you?' He replied, 'I'm an empowering leader'. Suitably impressed, I asked him what he meant. He said, 'Simple, I decide what needs to be done and then I get other people to do it'. We spent the next hour discussing the difference between delegation and empowerment!

Empowerment is not simply a matter of delegation in which you assign a task. Empowerment involves creating the opportunity for individuals and groups to contribute to defining and shaping their response to the task. People must have the latitude to contribute to decisions based on what they think should be done. They want to work in an environment that both builds their ability to perform a task or complete an assignment and promotes a sense of self-confidence in their judgement. If people feel ownership of their achievements they will work well for you and exercise personal accountability.

Just do it?

For example, if you say to someone 'I want you to do this or that', they may comply, but will often also instinctively resist you and harbour a negative feeling, such as 'but, I don't want to do it' or 'Why should I?' Throughout the course of your development, the chances are that you felt resentment when someone told you to do something.

Nothing has changed!

Throughout a typical working day, people build up resistance to being told what to do. Leaders who understand this can take account of this automatic negative reaction and overcome it by taking an approach based on dialogue. A more constructive strategy would be to approach the task with 'I was thinking we should do this, what do you think?' Alternatively, you could split the resistance into three by saying, 'I was thinking we could do this, or this, or do that. Which would you do?' This simple paradigm reduces resistance. People want to feel competent and contribute to decisions that involve their participation. If you focus on building up constructive dialogues, people are more likely to support you.

The paradox of power

There is a real paradox in exercising power — your power as a leader increases as you give it away. Notice that this is not the same as giving up your power. As I already established in chapter 2, as a leader you remain ultimately responsible for decisions made and actions that need to be taken. Research has consistently shown, however, that when people feel they can influence a decision and exercise a level of control, they invest emotionally in the outcome. Shared power leads to higher job satisfaction and increases performance throughout the organisation. Once people are treated as equals and can see the wins in a relationship, sharing power further communicates respect and trust. People who feel capable of influencing their circumstances are more ready to own their responsibilities. They are also more strongly connected to their leaders and more motivated to contribute value.

Have your cake and accomplish something too

In the 1950s, a cake-mix company learned the value of psychological wins when sales fell after they added dehydrated eggs to their mixes so that the customer only had to add milk. The manufacturer had been convinced that the convenience of having the egg already in the mix would be attractive to busy bakers. So why was there a drop in sales? It occurred because adding the egg made customers feel as if they were making the cake from scratch and doing something valuable for their families. In a more recent example from *The Wall Street Journal*, on 7 March 2001, Hamburger Helper said, 'The food industry obsessed for years with making products ever readier to eat, has had a revelation: Americans want to do a bit, but just a bit, of actual cooking'. The article went on to note that although most convenient foods could be cooked in a microwave oven, 'the microwave chef is left with little sense of accomplishment'. Hamburger Helper delivers the win of a fast meal and the feeling that you've prepared it yourself.[27]

FOCUS ON ALLOWING OTHERS TO TAKE THE LEAD IN SETTING THEIR OWN GOALS

Rather than dictating the terms and methods of people's development, your aim should be to focus on allowing others to take the lead in setting their own goals. You should point to problems without immediately offering a solution. For example, try saying: 'This is what I was thinking of doing and this is what I'm trying to achieve. These are the downsides and the upsides, what do you think?' This approach is effective because people come away feeling valued, thinking, 'I understand this. This person values my opinion and I get on well with him or her'.

Being inclusive and open creates positive emotions (emotional capital) that allows you to control a situation far more effectively.

Building emotional capital

Emotional capital, then, is built by positive emotion, which, in turn, supports high performance. Positive emotions address fundamental needs — affiliation, involvement, recognition and accomplishment — that people have in the workplace. These, and a range of other emotions and psychological forces at work within partners, affect people's relationships, including their business ones.

Although our discussion has focused on the horizontal dimension of business relationships (your internal stakeholders) the same principles can be applied for the vertical dimension of your business. They include the **PEOPLE NEED THE OPPORTUNITY TO EXPERIENCE WINS OF SOME KIND** relationships that you have with your external stakeholders, such as customers, suppliers, vendors, distributors, strategic partners, board of directors, financial institutions, and investors that make up your relationship network. Your job is to build reserves of emotional capital by developing highly productive relationships that get people working together — up, down and across your business towards common goals.

Summary

Relationship skills is a strategy that creates mutual wins for all partners in a business, and involves treating people as equals. It is a high-involvement, collaborative model that can be contrasted with other models emphasising transactional, paternalistic and adversarial relationships. Partnership involves the conscious decision to distribute power among all individuals with a stake in the business.

To be successful in a job, people need the opportunity to experience wins of some kind. Wins involve people feeling that they belong, are accepted and valued, and have the skills and inner resources needed to be successful. It also involves providing people with the autonomy and freedom to make choices, set goals and contribute to decisions. Sharing power increases the trust quotient, and people who feel capable of influencing their circumstances are more ready to take greater initiative and ownership. They are more strongly connected to their leaders and more motivated to contribute real value.

Relationships represent a unique strategic asset and are the primary source of emotional capital in an organisation. Managing them well is critical for building real competitive advantage in your business.

Building emotional capital

Strategies for developing relationship skills

- ☑ Strengthen your belief that people are basically your equals and interact with them on equal terms.

- ☑ Treat your people as partners and create rewarding wins for them.

- ☑ Identify individuals in your relationship network and develop a sense of ownership for cultivating and maintaining a quality connection.

- ☑ Empower your people by creating the opportunity for individuals and groups to contribute to defining and shaping a response to a task.

- ☑ Focus on building up constructive dialogues with people about direction and decisions.

- ☑ Promote positive emotions by addressing people's fundamental need for affiliation, involvement, recognition and accomplishment.

- ☑ Demonstrate care and respect for each of your people.

- ☑ Ensure they receive recognition or praise each week.

- ☑ Regularly encourage their personal and professional development.

What lies before us and what lies behind us are small matters compared to what lies within us. And when we bring what is within out into the world, miracles happen.

Henry David Thoreau

Empathic connection is the spark that drives sales, energises productive, creative teams and makes leadership talent dance.

Martyn Newman

8 Empathy

Interestingly, empathy is often the second characteristic that differentiates the genders — with women scoring higher in empathy than men. In our studies, all leaders scored higher in empathy than the average. When we look at some additional studies, however, particularly those measuiring transformational leadership — empathy was ranked as the highest score.[28] In other words, when successful leaders are rated against two criteria — the ability to empower others and be dynamic innovators — and when other factors, such as age and years of experience, are controlled, transformational leaders are distinguished by the ability to empathise with others. These superstar leaders also scored higher than the others in self-confidence, self-reliance, and optimism, but empathy remained the most important factor in distinguishing this group. Empathy represents one of the most important dynamic emotional competencies differentiating star performing leaders from the rest.

Empathy is often misunderstood — many people confuse it with sympathy. Steven Stein suggests that sympathy, while a valid emotion, refers to how you feel about someone else's misfortune, whereas empathy, on the other hand, shows that you understand how the other person feels. In other words, empathy is not about being warm and fuzzy, but about demonstrating that you can see the world from another person's point of view. This involves two dimensions: a cognitive dimension — understanding the task that other people must perform — and an emotional dimension — acknowledging the humanity of others by knowing your stakeholders as people and recognising and validating their emotional experience.

EVERYONE HAS A SHARE OR INTEREST IN THE SUCCESS OF YOUR BUSINESS AND IS LOOKING FOR POSITIVE OUTCOMES

I've come to recognise that in business all of your relationships are actually partner relationships. That is, everyone has a share or interest in the success of your business and is looking for positive outcomes. Once you discover what those outcomes are and what role you play in delivering them, you are on your way to a productive relationship. To tune in to what those interests really are, and their connection to the emotional gratifications I spoke about in chapter 3, is the key to moving your business relationships from contacts to connections.

The ability to empathise with others lets you grasp the emotional dimension of a business situation and create resonant connections with others. Once you have read the emotions of other people accurately, you are able to align with them to achieve productive outcomes. Well-developed empathy skills enable you to read the emotions inherent in each interpersonal exchange and allow you to build emotional capital by engaging with others to achieve win–win outcomes. By tuning in to people's feelings it is possible to move them in a positive direction. As Daniel Goleman suggests, 'When a leader triggers resonance, you can read it in people's eyes: They're engaged and they light up.'[29]

In other words, empathy allows you to create and maintain happy, productive relationships by focusing on the whole person as well as the tasks he or she must perform. In this way, you build emotional capital in the business by creating both compelling connections between yourself and your partners, and by creating a reservoir of goodwill and generosity that you can draw from when the pressure is on.

Of course, this assumes that you've developed your interpersonal relationship skills, conducted the groundwork necessary to establish connections with your people and have some understanding of how your team can help you to accomplish your goals. Before you can achieve your goals, however, you need to help your people achieve what they want.

Strategy one — focus on the cognitive dimension

To develop empathy in the workplace, you should focus first on the cognitive dimension.

Being more than 'Mr Nice Guy'

People often consider that empathy is really just about 'being nice' to people and, as such, has limited relevance in a competitive commercial environment. Although the business case for being warm and friendly to customers is well established, the primary power of empathy in the business context is actually cognitive. It's about how well you really understand what people are trying to achieve and the tasks they must perform.

Very often, leaders in positions of authority attempt to communicate to their people that they understand the particular challenges facing them, when, in reality, they don't. To grasp the experience of another you have to take the time to get to know what someone has to do, otherwise you run the risk of losing credibility. The more you are able to communicate accurately that you understand what your people are trying to achieve and what challenges they face in performing their tasks, the more constructively they will work for you and do the things you want them to do.

Remember — where you stand determines what you see

I commented in the previous chapter on the importance of looking for similarities between you and other people in order to set up collaborative relationships. Empathy requires that you take that a step further and actually try to place yourself emotionally in another person's situation. It's true that where we stand determines what we see, and effective leaders are adept at looking at things from a number of perspectives.

Mahatma Gandhi, for example, knew what had to be done to assist the villagers of India to improve their conditions. However, he felt he still did not empathise fully with the difficulties of living in a village. He had been talking and giving advice on village work without personally coming to grips with the difficulties of village work. Therefore, in 1936, at the age of sixty-five, Gandhi — who, at the time was India's most prominent leader — went to live in a typical Indian village with no running water, electricity, or paved roads. This was more than a gesture; it was a search to deepen his empathy.[30]

Closer to home, and certainly less significant, was the decision made by the management of a national engineering company who went into receivership after it lost a major contractor. Overnight, the firm, a manufacturer of engine components, lost a fifth of its revenue source, a loss that would typically have resulted in job cuts. In a strategy to avoid this, the board implemented a 10 per cent pay cut for all staff, fixed for 12 months, which it correctly believed would be supported by staff and the unions. However, it was their second decision that illustrates the company's very real interest in empathising with its staff. It was well aware that the pay cut would significantly effect staff, but more than that, it acknowledged that senior staff on management salaries were more likely to ride out the year with less pressure. Thus, in a move that conveyed both unity and the desire to truly share the experience, all members of the executive management team agreed to a salary cut of 15 per cent. Like the decision of Gandhi's to enter into the villager's world, so, too, did the management team feel a keen responsibility to show by its actions that it shared the staff's experience.

Of course, it isn't necessary to have first-hand knowledge of other people's experience to be empathetic. However, to develop effective connections with customers, both internal and external ones, it is at least necessary to imagine what it would be like to share their experience. This is known as 'shared state theory'. By sharing someone's experience, you establish the common ground essential to building rapport and achieving things effectively with other people. It's the emotional glue that creates interpersonal connections, establishes trust and relationship loyalty, and builds emotional capital.

Of course, it's not always easy for everybody. If it's not possible for you to stand somewhere else and see the world from another's perspective, then at least ask someone what they see and listen to their view. Do it regularly!

A short course in listening to get people talking

Perhaps it's so obvious that you haven't really thought about it, but the most powerful step to overcoming resistance is listening. As Daniel Goleman put it, 'listening well, the key to empathy, is … crucial to competence in communicating'.

According to a study conducted by John Haas and Chris Arnold in *The Journal of Business Communication* (April 1995), listening skills account for about a third of people's evaluations of whether or not someone they work with is an effective communicator. Active listening skills build rapport between people, create a positive climate for revealing important information and create an effective influence base. Active listening provides you with the information you need to gain the willing cooperation of others and allows you to confirm a situation before you waste time and effort attempting to solve the wrong issue. Like all of us, people who feel understood take more responsibility for themselves and are, overall, less defensive.

As a psychologist I've discovered that there is really no substitute for positive face-to-face interactions. Leaders create a trusting environment by the example they set through listening. If you want people to trust you, and if you want to build a climate of trust in your organisation, the listening-to-talk ratio has to be weighted in favour of listening. People need to feel that their voice counts.

There are a series of well-documented behaviours that comprise the essential steps to listening well and building empathic connections. Here is a short road map for creating effective emotional connections with others to build the inner side of business.

Step 1 — attention please ladies and gentlemen

The most obvious challenge to listening well is simple inattention. External factors — such as pressure schedules and multi-tasking — distract you, preventing you from giving your full attention to someone. There are also internal factors that make you inattentive — such as fatigue, passing premature judgement (approving or disapproving of the other person's statement), preparing your rebuttal, advising or offering premature reassurance. For example, imagine someone confiding in you, 'I'm unsure if I can manage this account'. If you're like most you probably respond immediately with, 'Don't worry, you'll be fine'. On the surface, reassurance like this can look like you're being helpful, but, offering reassurance prematurely is, in reality, often a way of avoiding the emotional demand that goes with exploring the person's situation. The first step in listening well, then, involves making a commitment to suspend your own agenda for a few moments, however important, and learning to focus your attention on the person in front of you and their agenda.

Step 2 — a posture of involvement

In practice, empathy begins with active listening and listening begins with being attentive. 'Attending' involves giving your physical attention to another person by listening to them describing their experience. People tend to think of communication as a verbal process, however, most psychological research estimates that 85 per cent of our communication is nonverbal. For example, good eye contact is an effective way of showing interest and also of picking up on another person's facial messages. By contrast, when you look away or down too often you will be perceived as being bored or uninterested. An open body posture and acceptable interpersonal space lets another person know that you are interested in what they are saying.

Consider developing a body posture of involvement. You've heard the expression, 'they were on the edge of their seats'. It suggests that when we are engaged with what's going on we display a body posture that moves towards the stimulus. In other words, when you want to communicate that you are listening to someone, lean towards the person. This conveys acceptance and that you consider what the person has to say as important. Similarly, the expression, 'he gave them the cold shoulder', reflects a posture of indifference or rejection. This highlights the importance of facing the person you are speaking with and making appropriate eye contact. These practices communicate genuine interest and respect.

In addition, become aware of your voice. Appropriate tone, volume and rate of verbal responses can enhance effective listening. Verbal tones create an emotional atmosphere. Generally, if you mimic the tone, volume and rate of the verbal responses of the person you are talking to, he or she will be more likely to feel understood. The tone of your voice can change from a low to a high tone, or from a relaxed to a tense tone. The optimum tone is one that is produced and heard without straining. The rate of your speech involves how many words you use in a response and also the frequency and duration of pauses between comments. To demonstrate that you really want to listen to another you can pause slightly when they stop speaking to see if they wish to continue. A rapid speech rate response can increase the tension in a conversation that may be unwanted. By contrast, slowing your speech rate down has the effect of taking the emotional temperature down, too. These are the physical mechanics of listening, but what a person wants most of all from someone who listens to them is psychological presence.

Step 3 — a question's worth a thousand words

Psychological presence is communicated by a single-minded focus on actively facilitating the process of disclosure. Once eye contact is established and your smile and body posture convey that you are giving the other person your full attention, 'use minimal encouragers' — responses that use a combination of verbal and nonverbal cues — to encourage the other person to keep talking. Minimal encouragers imply that 'I'm with you' or 'Please go on'.

In addition to a warm smile or a simple nod of the head to indicate you're listening, verbal encouragers include brief affirming words such as: 'Sure...', '...then?', '...ummm', '...oh?'

OPEN QUESTIONS ARE MORE THOUGHT PROVOKING THAN CLOSED ONES

or 'I hear you'. Another kind of encourager involves repeating the prominent word in, or last word of, the sentence just spoken, along with maintaining an inquiring tone of voice that invites clarification. Remember, listening doesn't mean not speaking. By using minimal encouragers you communicate that you are with the speaker, encouraging him or her to continue.

An open invitation to talk, however briefly, is like a gift to a colleague or client. Good questions create this invitation and facilitate conversations.

Communication experts differentiate between two types of questions: 'open' and 'closed'. Closed questions, such as 'Have you finished the brief for the sales team?' or 'Are you the new technician?' can usually be answered in a few words or, more often, with a straight 'yes' or 'no'. They are useful for eliciting a concrete commitment or specific piece of information, but they also shut down dialogue. They often begin with, 'Have...?', 'Did...?', 'Are ...?' or 'Is ...?'

Open questions are more thought provoking than closed ones. They provide an invitation to a colleague or client to express and explore his or her ideas, allowing the listener to take an active interest in what the other has to say. Open questions, such as 'How are things coming along in your department since we spoke last time?', help to expand a conversation. They also help people to elaborate on a point of discussion, for example, 'Could you tell me more about that?' or 'What's your view of the new proposal?' Open questions prompt open-ended responses and often begin with: 'Who ...?', 'What ...?', 'Where ...?', 'Why ...?' or 'How ...?'

By asking questions, particularly open questions, you prompt people to express themselves. Questions for clarification allow the listener to take an active interest in what the other has to say and help to expand the discussion.

Asking your people about what they would like to achieve is simple and direct. Of course, it is easier to do this with people you already have a good relationship with, but it should be done early in a business relationship. Tom Richardson, Augusto Vidaurreta and Tom Gorman, from the Systems Consulting Group, have suggested adopting a collaborative approach that emphasises wins for both people in a relationship:

> Here are the wins I would like to achieve, provided that we can do business together and get a relationship going. And here are some of the wins that I believe you would get out of the relationship. What I would like to do is learn more about your potential wins and maybe modify my own. How does that sound to you?[31]

This approach sets up an agenda that allows you to work towards creating wins so that everyone feels like a winner.

Step 4 — pause and paraphrase

The skill of listening well also involves the ability to respond reflectively. In a reflective response, the listener restates the content of what the person said in a way that demonstrates understanding and acceptance. Before rushing to respond to what a person has said, it is often helpful to pause and paraphrase what it is you think you've heard. A good paraphrase is concise, reflects only the content of the speaker's message, and involves using the speaker's own words without parroting them. Paraphrasing not only reduces the chances of a misunderstanding occurring, but also suggests that you have paid careful attention and taken the person seriously.

When paraphrasing, as you are trying to feed back to the person what you think they just said, so, your voice should reflect an inquiring tone. Begin with a tentative 'lead in', such as, 'Sounds like…', 'So, what you seem to be saying is…' or 'So, what I'm hearing is…' Continue by identifying the emotion (if there is one expressed) by making comments such as, '…you're concerned…' Then, link it to the content of what the person is referring to, such as saying, '…about meeting that deadline'. Finish with a 'check-out'. A 'check-out' takes the form of a closed question and invites a confirming response, such as, 'Is that right?'

Active listening together with empathic reflection allows you to accurately identify what the customer's real concerns are and focus on generating a more productive response.

When being 'talented' isn't enough

Andrew S was the head of research and development of a large pharmaceutical company that I worked with several years ago. At the time, the company was involved in a merger and all of the senior management were being repositioned in the new structure.

Valued for his enormous talent, incisive, penetrating mind and personal creativity, Andrew was larger than life and tended to dominate any project in which he got involved. In Andrew's mind, he was simply ensuring high standards were maintained and that his department delivered the best possible result.

Unfortunately, his people frequently complained that they often felt overwhelmed by the strength of his approach and didn't feel that their contribution was particularly valued. Unfortunately, Andrew had inadvertently created an intimidating climate in which people felt devalued and unheard. As a result, they tended to back off from contributing original ideas.

After completing his EQ assessment, Andrew was surprised to discover that while he was valued for his intelligence and innovation, he was also viewed as overwhelming, a bad listener and, at times, unnecessarily critical. Together we examined his drive to explore new ideas and he explained the satisfaction he gained from 'putting the puzzle together'. He also came to consider that his strength of character may also make it difficult for others to feel they have much to contribute. He certainly recognised the important role his team played in delivering results, and admitted to feeling frustrated with them at times for failing to offer much at team briefings.

As we explored a little further, Andrew acknowledged that he often couldn't be bothered with small talk and was impatient with people when they took too long to make their point. I suggested to him that if he wanted to be the team leader he obviously wanted to be, then his job was to draw out the strength of his team and focus their collective energy and skill on creating new products. To do this he would need to connect with his team more effectively. Of course, I recommended that the best strategy for doing this was to develop his empathy skills.

Andrew had never considered empathy as an influencing strategy and the idea of increasing his ability to understand and influence others appealed to him.

Make talent dance

I first appealed to Andrew's native curiosity and suggested that he adopt an approach towards people that aimed at discovering more of what they were about. To do this he would need to put aside his own agenda, suspend judgement and focus on listening to others without interrupting. Typical of Andrew's enthusiasm, he wanted to practise this new approach right away and immediately began listening more attentively, exploring other people's points of view using the active listening skills I'd modelled for him. It took him a while to learn to curb his natural enthusiasm for bouncing back with his own ideas, but by focusing intently on making sure the other person felt heard before offering his view, he quickly discovered that other people were warming up to him.

He also changed the way he ran meetings by adopting the role of facilitator rather than director of the discussion. He would systematically listen to others, solicit their views and occasionally reflect back what he had just heard without judging it. Andrew also discovered that he didn't necessarily need to agree with what another person was saying in order to validate a different point of view from his own.

Like all new skills, it took practice, but he noticed that his approach had a very positive effect on others. His people began offering their own ideas more freely and were less tentative about making humourous remarks.

To Andrew's surprise, the sort of changes he was looking for came much more quickly than he could have imagined. He discovered that, as a strategy, listening systematically enabled him to connect more personally with colleagues and created a new climate for the open exchange of fresh ideas. Quite quickly, this had a dramatic impact on the energy and productivity of his entire department. As a leader he had discovered it's emotional capital that makes talent dance.

Building emotional capital

In the real, day-to-day world of interactions within your business, developing an authentic psychological presence and asking good questions usually saves time and enables you to get on well with others. This is the key to building and sustaining profitable relationships. If you're hearing strong views being expressed without good reason, you may consider saying, 'You may be right, but I'd like to understand more about this. What, specifically leads you to feel that ...?' If you become aware of a strong negative reaction in others, you might respond by saying, 'I may have misunderstood, but when you said ... I had the impression you were feeling ... If that's true, I'd like to understand what's concerning you about that'. Often, when people share ideas or opinions you may have the internal reaction of, 'that's just stupid'. You may or may not be right, but the important thing is to suspend the impulse to react abruptly and dismiss the idea. Instead, take a moment to inquire further and ask, 'In what way do you feel this idea would be good for business?'

Above all, learn to suspend judgement and to develop an attitude of curiosity. Understanding the cognitive dimension of empathy helps you to focus on the importance of gathering a sense of what others are feeling, experiencing, and intending. By adopting an attitude of genuine curiosity and by suspending judgement you focus on getting to the heart of the other person's experience. By keeping your eyes engaged with the speaker, asking questions for clarification, remaining open and paraphrasing what you hear, you overcome resistance and create the conditions for effective cooperation.

Leaders high in empathy understand the task their people must perform and sense the feelings, needs and perspectives of others. Putting yourself in the other person's shoes amounts to commonsense — particularly if you want to engage with them to sell an idea or a product, or simply to communicate respect and foster a collaborative relationship. But like so much commonsense, it's easier to ignore than to practise.

Strategy 2 — the emotional dimension

The second dimension of empathy is more emotive. It involves treating people as human beings by validating their experience. Both the cognitive and emotional dimensions of empathy work together as you get a fix on the feelings as well as the facts that affect people's experience. You will build the best relationships by getting to know your stakeholders not only as stakeholders, but as people with thoughts and feelings similar, although not identical, to your own.

The person in the role

To engage this dimension of empathy, Richardson and Vidaurreta suggest that you put yourself in the other person's place by asking yourself questions such as, 'What are this person's skills, knowledge, and areas of expertise?', 'What are his nominal and actual roles in the organisation?', 'What are her foremost job-related worries?' or 'What are her most important worries off the job?'

PUTTING YOURSELF IN THE OTHER PERSON'S SHOES AMOUNTS TO COMMONSENSE

In other words, take the time to consider other relationships in the person's business life, and, when relevant, his or her personal life. This can help you to understand the pressures, prospects and risks he or she faces and the goals he or she is trying to achieve. For example, Bob Galvin, CEO and founder of Motorola, described how his father once looked out at the assembly line of women working in his plant and thought, 'These are all like my own mom — they have kids, homes to take care of, people who need them'. Galvin went on to describe how it motivated his father to work hard to give them a better life because he saw his mother in all of them. 'That's how it all begins,' Galvin suggests, 'with fundamental respect and empathy.'[32]

Building emotional connections with stakeholders isn't rocket science, nor is it mysterious or manipulative. But if you want to build emotional capital, you don't just let relationships happen. You adopt emotional intelligence as a strategy and make them happen. Taking an active interest in your stakeholders as people enables you to create more rewarding wins for them, fluid interactions and longer term relationships. Realising these aims along with the resultant growth and profitability — are the goals of every principle and practice of building emotional capital.

The way to a person's heart

You'll remember that I commented in chapter 3 that the way to a person's heart is through the stomach — you know, that satisfying a person's fundamental needs is the best way to win their heart and mind. Well, it strikes me that empathy is by far the best strategy for understanding and meeting a person's fundamental emotional needs.

Heinz Kohut, who I also referred to in chapter 6, suggested that at the psychological level people have two essential needs: to be understood and to be admired; however, the most fundamental need is to be understood. In other words, if you can communicate that you understand another person's experience you will build a valuable connection and he or she will work well for you, buy from you and enter into business with you. Goleman refers to the experience of two or more people being on the same wavelength emotionally as 'synchronous vibration'. When people feel this connection they are comfortable sharing their thoughts, feelings and ideas — they are 'in sync'.

The most interesting person on earth

Management guru Tom Peters puts it simply when he suggests that great leaders really are 'there'. What he means is that effective leaders really are intensely concentrated on you. People should come away from talking to you convinced that they are the most interesting person on earth. You achieve this by focusing on the emotional connection with people.

In my experience there are three steps for developing and applying the emotional dimension of empathy and developing 'in sync' connections.

Step one — reflect the context and content

Step one involves demonstrating a genuine interest in understanding the context and content of the other person's experience by applying active listening strategies, and by simply repeating or reflecting back to the person what you've heard.

Take Charlotte, for example. After completing the first term of her MBA, Charlotte was devastated to discover she had received 79 per cent on her exam. Despite the fact she was slotting her studies in around an already demanding job as junior partner in an accounting firm, and raising two-year-old twins with her equally stretched husband, as a high achiever she felt anything less than 85 per cent was inadequate. Charlotte was so distressed when she received her results that she arranged a meeting with her managing partner to discuss her decision to withdraw from the course. Her manager, Therese, listened as Charlotte spoke of her disappointment and anger at herself for not doing better, her concern that she was juggling so many responsibilities and the myriad ways she felt she was letting down the team at work. Finally, she told Therese that the only way to manage all of this was to withdraw from the course. Therese listened until Charlotte had finished and then said to her:

> *You are certainly juggling a lot of important priorities right now — being a mother, a partner, and an employee, as well as a student. I'm getting the sense that in trying so hard to make them work together, you're actually seeing that maybe you're only human. It sounds like you want to prioritise your responsibilities by removing the one that is of lesser importance to you, and right now, that seems like your MBA.*

In several sentences Therese captured the essence of Charlotte's message and in relaying it to Charlotte she was able to confirm that she had understood the key points. In other words, Therese had taken a moment to check that she'd understood the context and content of Charlotte's experience and summarised it.

Step two — identify the thoughts and feelings

The next step in empathic listening involves reflecting the thoughts, and particularly the feelings, that a person appears to be expressing. This is known as 'interchangeable empathy'. For example, after Charlotte agreed that Therese's summary was spot-on, Therese followed with a reflection on the other part of Charlotte's statements — the emotional content:

> *From what you have said, it sounds that you are completely overwhelmed with trying to make all the parts of your life work together right now. I know that you like to give everything 110 per cent and you're frustrated that you are unable to achieve the standards you set for yourself.*

In saying this, Therese was showing her junior colleague that she understood the emotional turmoil Charlotte was experiencing right now, and that she understood not just the words, but the emotional impact of Charlotte's situation at a deeper level.

Step three — the unspoken feelings

Given that Therese and Charlotte had worked together for some time and knew each other quite well, Therese chose to offer a deeper level of support. There is a further dimension to empathy in which you add to your reflection a tentative interpretation that reflects the unspoken feelings. This is called 'additive empathy'. For example, Therese continued by saying, 'Since your exam mark came back, I'm sensing that you feel like you've failed in all of the things that matter most to you and you're questioning whether you are capable of seeing this through.' Here, Therese picks up on the deeper feelings that Charlotte may be feeling and puts them into words that capture that experience. Of course, it may not always be appropriate to take the discussion to this level, and you certainly want to be confident that you're reading the situation accurately. In other words, always offer this level of reflection tentatively, with a questioning tone that provides the opportunity to validate or dismiss it. However, if you're on the money, you will have established a very firm connection with the other person.

EMPATHY REQUIRES BEING ABLE TO READ ANOTHER'S EMOTIONS AT A HIGHER LEVEL

Sensing what another is feeling without them saying so, captures the essence of empathy. People may not often tell us in words what they feel, but they do communicate their feelings in their tone of voice, their facial expression and other nonverbal ways. At the very least, empathy requires being able to read another's emotions at a higher level. It entails sensing and responding to a person's unspoken concerns or feelings. According to Goleman, empathy is our social radar and in business it is at this level of emotional exchange that we have the potential to make the most effective connections with other people. Emotions convey crucial information that transcends the content of the words used. They are part of the emotional economy that passes between people. This level of empathy requires you to go beneath the speaker's words and look for the real feelings that surround the person's experience.

What is it that compels people to act?

According to Maslow, people are moved to satisfy their needs. They have needs for safety and survival, to be loved and to belong, and needs for esteem and achievement. Even if these needs appear on the surface to be practical or simply functional, they are at their most basic level, emotional. Every time you are persuaded to engage in a new behaviour, you do so because you are motivated by the effects of emotion. Understanding the emotional needs of your people and customers, and working hard to satisfy them is the surest way to motivate them to action. And if satisfying a customer's needs has anything to do with purchasing your products or buying-in to your leadership, then it's of enormous interest to you and your business.

Robert Peterson, marketing professor at the University of Texas, specialises in understanding the factors that determine customer satisfaction. After more than 100 research studies he has determined that the connection between customer satisfaction and repeat business involves establishing an emotional link between the customer and everyone the customer comes into contact with at your company.[33]

In other words, your customers, internal and external, are human beings, and they possess all the complexities of being human. You will build the most valuable relationships by relating to all of your customers, not only as stakeholders, but also as people.

From good to great

In my view, responding to people with empathy is actually the origin of compassion — which literally means 'to feel with'. In the end, as a leader, it's empathy and compassion that connect you with people and enable you to establish valuable connections with all your customers.

Some years ago I had the opportunity of trekking in Nepal, close to the Tibetan border. When people greet each other in Nepal they do so by saying 'Namaste'. In the east of Tibet they say 'Tashi deley'. Both greetings convey a similar meaning: 'I honour the greatness in you. I honour the place in your heart where lives your courage, honour, love, hope, and dreams. I honour that place in you where, if you are at that place in you and I am at that place in me, there is only one of us.' Robert Cooper and Ayman Sawaf, leading researchers in the field of emotional intelligence, tell the story of one day visiting a village in Tibet where a group of children greeted them with 'Tashi deley'. Their children's father asked them to teach them a word in English. They thought for a moment then replied, 'In America, when we greet each other we say 'Hello'. 'Hello!' shouted the children, beaming, 'Hello! Hello!' Then something happened that Cooper and Sawaf say they will never forget. One of the youngest boys approached them and asked, 'In America, when people say 'hello', do they honour the greatness in each other?'[34]

I'm convinced that your effectiveness as a leader will be defined by your capacity to bring out the greatness in others. This is not about being warm and fuzzy. It's the challenge of being able to establish a solid platform of mutual respect and empathic connection with people. This connection is essential to leading a team, communicating across cultural and sub-cultural divides, developing talent, engaging customers and moving your people and your business from good to great.

Summary

Of all the competencies that set you apart as a great leader, your capacity for empathy is the most fundamental. No matter how you look at it, relationships with all stakeholders are the greatest asset in any business — whether they are relationships with employees, managers, partners, suppliers, vendors or customers. And relationships depend on positive emotional connections. Your capacity for seeing or experiencing another's situation from their perspective lets you grasp the emotional dimensions of a business situation.

As a strategy for building emotional capital, empathy involves understanding the tasks that people are trying to perform, listening well, asking strategic questions and identifying the emotional needs that direct the behaviour of people. If you get it right, you will greatly enhance your capacity to influence others to achieve what is impossible without their commitment.

Building emotional capital

Strategies for developing empathy

☑ Practise active listening:

- Pause and give people your full attention.

- Make soft, natural eye contact.

- Lean forward — add a warm smile and a nod of the head and provide minimal encouragers.

☑ Ask clear, open questions that draw out the person's point of view and feelings.

☑ Paraphrase what you have heard using an inquiring tone that reflects the content and the emotion contained in the message.

☑ Suspend judgement and develop an attitude of curiosity.

☑ Take an active interest in your stakeholders as people and create more rewarding wins for them.

☑ Make your people feel like they are the most interesting people on earth by demonstrating empathic reflection:

- Demonstrate a genuine interest in understanding the context and content of the other person's experience.

- Practise 'interchangeable empathy' — reflect the thoughts and particularly the feelings that a person appears to be expressing.

- Practise 'additive empathy' — add to your reflection a tentative interpretation that reflects the unspoken feelings.

☑ Look for the greatness in others and support it by providing feedback to others at every opportunity.

9 Conclusion

Emotional capitalism is a leadership philosophy for the twenty-first century. Today, you and your business are competing on the basis of emotion and imagination. Your task is to capture the energy and imagination of the people inside and around your business and move this energy forward to create wealth in the fullest sense of the word.

It takes real emotional strength to lead. While becoming an emotional capitalist isn't easy, being intelligent about your emotions is critical to your success as a leader. Your personal level of emotional capital will determine your capacity to inspire or demoralise others.

Paying attention to developing your emotional intelligence and using the strategies described in these chapters, will equip you to build the emotional wealth necessary to sustain your personal energy, enthusiasm and commitment. These strategies will also enable you to develop and maintain the level of positive, focused energy that your people require to invest intelligently at work.

It is the energy and enthusiasm that your people bring to work that will determine the capacity of your business to create products, solve problems and deliver superior service. In the end, your vision can only be realised through them.

If leadership is ultimately the art of accomplishing extraordinary things with ordinary people, then building emotional capital is how you achieve it.

Appendix

The emotional capital inventory (ECi): measuring emotional capital

What is the Emotional Capital Inventory (ECi)? The ECi is a survey that measures your level of personal emotional capital quickly and accurately. It represents an innovation in the measurement of emotional intelligence and leadership behaviors. The ECi™ and ECi 360™ are an exciting advance in our ability to measure the building blocks that are scientifically linked to the behaviors of successful leaders.

As a reader of *Emotional Capitalists — The New Leaders* you may like to test-drive the Emotional Capital Inventory (ECi) for yourself. The 'Emotional Capital Inventory' measures your personal level of emotional capital quickly and accurately and delivers a summary report of your scores on the seven leadership competencies covered in this book, plus three additional competencies that also characterise effective leaders. To obtain your free promotional code simply email <contact@rochemartin.com>. The inventory can be accessed online at <www.emotionalcapitalists.com>. Simply go to 'Discover your emotional capital', select 'Find out more', enter the promotional code, register your details and complete the inventory. Your report is generated by comparing your responses to thousands of professional people who have taken the test during the scientific development of the inventory. The average administration time is about ten minutes.

If your primary role as a leader is to create emotional wealth for competitive advantage, use this tool both to benchmark your own level of emotional capital and as a blueprint for developing your skills going forward.

The inventory is designed as a learning tool to assist you to understand and apply these particular EQ competencies to the challenges of being an effective leader. Of course, determining your scores on the ECi is at least a start in helping you to clarify and prioritise your development challenges.

If you'd like a more detailed roadmap to guide you, you can purchase the *Emotional Capital Report*. The report includes a full interpretation of your scores and provides specific coaching strategies you can immediately employ to develop and apply the vital leadership skills that achieve outstanding results. Simply visit <www.emotionalcapitalists.com> and purchase your personal *Emotional Capital Report*.

The ECi is also available in a multi-rater edition — the ECi 360™. The ECi 360™ uses an online multi-rater method and, through the combination of responses from colleagues, an individual's scores are compared to 'rater' scores to yield a gap analysis and an understanding of differences in self/other perception. A coaching section examines those particular factors where 'self' scores and 'rater' scores are significantly different and provides coaching strategies for improving leadership performance.

The emotional capitalist leadership system: building emotional capital

What is the Emotional Capitalist Leadership System? We know emotional intelligence is made up of flexible skills that can be learned. However, learning them quickly and efficiently to achieve real change is a tough challenge. Actually, more than twenty years of research has identified seven critical conditions that accelerate and sustain change in emotionally intelligent behaviours. The Emotional Capitalist Leadership System is a powerful, proven, seven-step process that leverages these seven conditions to maximise the development of emotional intelligence in leaders. Each step in the process is supported by a highly practical tool designed to break open the building blocks of emotional intelligence and accelerate learning. The system is scaleable and adaptable, and uses a combination of face-to-face and online modalities that enable teams in diverse geographical locations to build emotional capital together.

The Emotional Capitalist Leadership System (overleaf) comprises seven steps.

The emotional capitalist leadership system

STEPS	SUMMARY DESCRIPTION
New leaders seminar (1)	Dr Martyn Newman introduces the science of Emotional Intelligence and presents a compelling business case for its relationship to leadership success. He explores the research that has identified the seven dynamic emotions that drive leadership success and presents practical strategies for applying these immediately to achieve results.
EQ Assessment & Feedback (2)	Emotional Intelligence is benchmarked using the Emotional Capital Inventory— the international 'gold standard' for measuring EQ and leadership. Results are discussed using a propriety Transformational Assessment methodology. Dr Newman's research supporting the effectiveness of this process has been published by the American Psychological Association.
Report & Goal Setting (3)	Results are captured in the *Emotional Capital Report*— a 'highly individualised blueprint' for taking action to improve EQ and leadership competencies. The report captures the unique interplay of a number of ECi scores and integrates them into a leadership competency framework that identifies strengths, development opportunities and strategies for change.

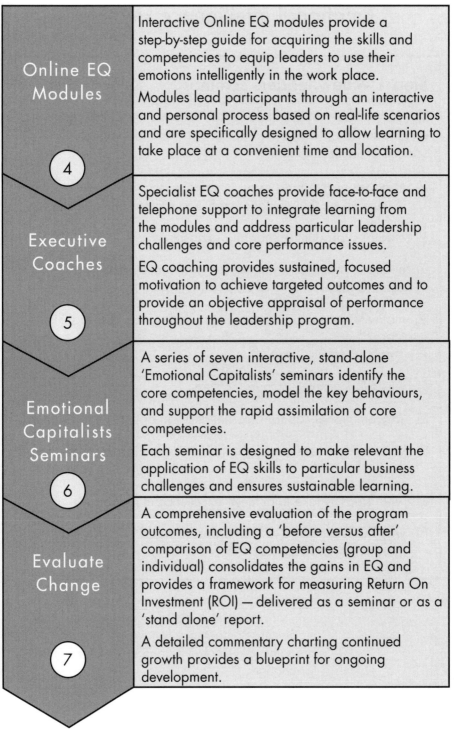

Online EQ Modules

4

Interactive Online EQ modules provide a step-by-step guide for acquiring the skills and competencies to equip leaders to use their emotions intelligently in the work place.

Modules lead participants through an interactive and personal process based on real-life scenarios and are specifically designed to allow learning to take place at a convenient time and location.

Executive Coaches

5

Specialist EQ coaches provide face-to-face and telephone support to integrate learning from the modules and address particular leadership challenges and core performance issues.

EQ coaching provides sustained, focused motivation to achieve targeted outcomes and to provide an objective appraisal of performance throughout the leadership program.

Emotional Capitalists Seminars

6

A series of seven interactive, stand-alone 'Emotional Capitalists' seminars identify the core competencies, model the key behaviours, and support the rapid assimilation of core competencies.

Each seminar is designed to make relevant the application of EQ skills to particular business challenges and ensures sustainable learning.

Evaluate Change

7

A comprehensive evaluation of the program outcomes, including a 'before versus after' comparison of EQ competencies (group and individual) consolidates the gains in EQ and provides a framework for measuring Return On Investment (ROI) — delivered as a seminar or as a 'stand alone' report.

A detailed commentary charting continued growth provides a blueprint for ongoing development.

Emotional intelligence keynote

Step 1 — new leaders seminar

Dr Martyn Newman, a world leader on emotional intelligence and leadership presents an inspirational look at the art and science of leadership that:

☑ engages participants in an interactive and thought-provoking discussion on the relevance of EQ to successful leadership

☑ creates a productive learning atmosphere

☑ provides practical strategies for immediately applying EQ to achieve results

☑ motivates people to want to improve their leadership skills.

The two-hour seminar explains:

☑ why EQ is important in leadership

☑ why emotional capital is essential as an approach to business

☑ what the business case is for EQ and what is in it for the time poor

☑ what steps to take to achieve excellence in leadership

☑ why EQ is attractive to the corporate world and why it is more important than IQ.

Step 2 — EQ assessment and feedback

All participants complete the Emotional Capital Inventory (ECi), which:

☑ is one of the most extensively developed and researched measures of emotional intelligence and leadership

☑ uses ten multidimensional factors specifically linked to effective leadership and representing the 5 general domains of EQ facilitates comparison across all validated models of emotional intelligence

☑ makes use of a large international normative database of 3240 professional people, including participants from Europe, Australia and the USA ensures a broad representation of leadership norms

☑ has very good statistical reliability and validity that provides increased confidence in the dependability and quality of the profile

☑ was developed with an international and multicultural focus.

In addition, participants complete the readily recognisable Myers Briggs Type Indicator (MBTI) to round out the profile.

Participants also have the option to complete an ECi 360 assessment, which gathers important information on how others rate the participant on EQ competencies.

Transformational assessment feedback

Transformational assessment (TA) is a practised procedure that aims to deliver information obtained from the ECi to maximise effective, positive behaviour change. TA is delivered by trained psychologists in a two-hour session in either a small group or one-on-one session. Transformational assessment:

☑ equips participants to be self-directed learners and to develop positive expectations of success

☑ reinforces and clarifies existing strengths, targets development needs and builds effective strategies to increase leadership competencies.

Step 3 — reporting and goal setting

The Emotional Capital Report provides professional people with a comprehensive interpretation of their leadership potential based upon their scores on the ECi.

The report integrates the ECi scores into a leadership competency framework that clearly identifies ten strengths and development opportunities along with practical strategies for change, including:

☑ self-awareness

☑ self-confidence

☑ self-reliance

☑ self-actualisation

☑ assertiveness

☑ relationship skills

☑ empathy

☑ flexibility

☑ self-control

☑ optimism.

Participants complete the session with a highly individualised blueprint for taking action to improve their EQ and leadership skills.

Step 4 — online EQ modules

The online EQ modules:

- ☑ are tried and tested in the workplace and are world-leading online EQ modules that use 'Intrusive Learning' techniques

- ☑ lead participants through a simple, interactive and personal process based on real-life scenarios that highlight the emotional skills essential to effective leadership performance

- ☑ are a series of dynamic interactive exercises that systematically build emotional intelligence — learning is delivered in concentrated, time-efficient, thirty-minute blocks

- ☑ are flexible and mobile, the modules are time-efficient, delivered via the internet and supported by a range of leading-edge technologies and coaching strategies, including intrusive learning.

Intrusive learning

Intrusive learning is designed to take the process of thinking and learning about the EQ module content away from the computer and into 'real life'. It ensures that learned behaviours are being practised and that module information is accessible — anywhere and anytime.

Intrusive learning uses two mechanisms:

- ☑ module-related questions delivered to mobile phones via SMS

- ☑ cheat sheets (summaries of module information) — available free of charge to registered corporate users in PDF format.

Step 5 — EQ executive coaching

EQ executive coaching is designed to support the e-learning modules and business objectives of the client company and individual participants.

Delivered by telephone or face-to-face, the coaching plan is tailored to individual needs.

RocheMartin-accredited coaches provide a reservoir of ideas, experience and information that support clients as they work their way through the stages of each EQ module.

Core performance issues are clarified and strategies developed to assist in the rapid assimilation of information and acquisition of core competencies.

EQ coaching provides the participant with sustained, focused motivation to achieve the targeted outcomes and an objective evaluation of performance throughout the learning experience.

EQ leadership and coaching guides

☑ coaching is supported by a series of guides that assist participants to identify the steps involved in acquiring the particular EQ skill they need and then progressing systematically towards mastery.

☑ modules and coaching sessions are tailored for individuals based upon their scores on the EQ Leadership & Coaching Report and feedback.

Step 6 — new leaders seminar

A series of seven interactive, stand-alone *Emotional Capitalists — The New Leaders* seminars designed to explore the seven dynamic emotions that drive leadership success.

The seminars model key behaviours and support the rapid assimilation of core skills.

Each seminar is designed to make the application of EQ skills relevant to particular business challenges and ensure sustainable learning.

The seven seminars include:

☑ relationship skills — building relationship capital

☑ empathy — creating partnerships across the business

☑ assertiveness — generating market-driven communications

☑ optimism — seizing opportunities — inoculating against

☑ setbacks

☑ self-actualisation — sustaining leadership for the long term

☑ self-confidence — creating high-performance environments

☑ self-reliance — creating and sustaining vision.

This is a cost-effective way to support the rapid assimilation of core competencies.

The seminars ensure sustainable learning and relevant application of skills to business challenges.

Step 7 — evaluate change

Evaluating change involves:

☑ a continuous and rigorous evaluation of each step in the program, ensuring accountability for behaviour change and sustainment of motivation for learning

☑ a comprehensive evaluation of program outcomes, including a 'before versus after' comparison of EQ competencies (group and individual) — it consolidates gains made in EQ and provides a framework for measuring return on investment (ROI)

☑ deliverance of the evaluation in a seminar or as a stand-alone report

☑ identification of outstanding opportunities for continued development and provision of recommendations to sustain growth.

Notes

1   AR Damasio, *Descartes' error: emotion, reason, and the human brain*, Putnam, New York, 1994. Damasio's other patients with prefrontal lobe deficits made disastrous financial, professional or ethical decisions, while still able to consider the pros and cons of their decisions. They were unable to sustain long-term intimate relationships, wasted money in unwise financial decisions and were incapable of sustaining mutually satisfying and effective interpersonal relationships.

2   J LeDoux, *The emotional brain*, Basic Books, New York, 1996. A powerful, yet highly readable explanation of the way emotional experiences can be mapped in different parts of the brain.

3   K Thomson, *Emotional capital: maximising the intangible assets at the heart of brand and business success*, Capstone,

Oxford, 1989. Thomson popularised the term Emotional Capital in English, but the idea actually draws on Benedicte Gendron's model in which she combined human capital theory and the emotional competencies from emotional intelligence models. In her emotional capital model (which in 2006 won a National Prize of the Academie Francaise) she stressed that emotional capital is essential to enable human capital formation and is crucial in human resources management in today's increasingly complex and competitive global workplace. In his work, Thomson identified the first two core elements of emotional capital. Here I introduce a third element critical to the role of leadership.

4   To date, the two leading models of emotional intelligence have been described by Reuven Bar-On in the *Emotional Quotient Inventory (EQ-i): Technical Manual*, Multi-Health Systems Inc., Toronto, Canada, 1997; and Daniel Goleman, *Emotional Intelligence*, Bantam Books, New York, 1995. At the most general level, both models share a common core of basic concepts that refer to the ability to recognise and regulate emotions in ourselves and in others. These abilities have suggested four major domains or meta-factors of EI that are shared by all the main variations of EQ theory: self-awareness, self-management, social awareness and social skills. The EQ domains of self-awareness and self-management appear to reflect what Howard Gardner (*Frames of Mind*, Basic Books, New York, 1983) explains in his conceptualisation of personal intelligences as 'intrapersonal intelligence'. The domains of social awareness and social skills, on the other hand, appear to fit with his definition of interpersonal intelligence. Bar-On prefers Gardner's terms to cluster a number of specific emotional and social competencies in his model. Similarly, Goleman clusters a number of competencies as self-management that Bar-On prefers to

separate into two clusters: adaptability and general mood. The Bar-On model also includes a domain labeled 'stress management' that is made up of two factors: impulse control, that best fits within Goleman's self-management cluster; and stress tolerance, which appears unique to the Bar-On model.

5   M Newman, *Emotional Capital Inventory: Technical Manual* (2007). The ECi has been used with corporate leaders from a number of specialist groups of professional people who may be regarded as leaders in their fields. These groups were chosen to examine the criterion validity of the ECi and whether the ECi had the ability to adequately identify those individuals regarded as leaders by their peers. A total of 100 leaders participated in the studies. When scores from these three leadership groups were combined, all scores were significantly higher than the average on all ECi scales. These finding are consistent with the theoretical and empirical basis upon which the ECi was constructed and confirm that the ECi is an ideal instrument to assess EQ as it supports effective leadership performance.

6   B Tracey, *Maximum achievement: strategies and skills that will unlock your hidden powers to succeed*, Fireside, New York, 1993.

7   M Gerber, *E-Myth mastery: the seven essential disciplines for building a world class company*, HarperCollins, New York, 2005.

8   A Watts, *Tao: the watercourse way*, Pantheon Books, New York, 1975.

9   H Gardner, *Learning minds*, Basic Books, New York, 1995.

10   J Welch, *Winning*, HarperCollins, New York, 2005.

11   L Harker and D Keltner, 'Expressions of positive emotion in women's college yearbook pictures and their relationship to personality and life outcomes across adulthood', *Journal of personality and social psychology*, no. 80, 2001, pp. 112–124.

12   M Seligman's books, *Learned optimism* (1991), *What you can change ... and what you can't* (1994), *The optimistic child* (with Reivich, Jaycox and Gillham) (1995) and *Authentic happiness: using the new positive psychology to realize you potential for lasting fulfillment* (2002) provide definitive statements on the subject of how to build optimism as a positive skill.

13   L Boldt, *How to be, do, or have anything: a practical guide to creative empowerment*, Lightening, Santa Barbara, 2001.

14   M Csikszentmihalyi, *Flow: the psychology of optimal experience*, Harper & Row, New York, 1990.

15   M Ryan and EL Deci, 'Self-determination theory and the facilitation of intrinsic motivation, social development, and well-being', *American psychologist*, vol. 55, no. 1, January 2000, pp. 68–78.

16   R McAfee-Brown, *Creative dislocation: the movement of grace*, Abingdon, Nashville, 1980. I am indebted to my teacher, Robert McAfee-Brown, Emeritus Professor at the Pacific School of Religion, Berkeley, California, who first persuaded me that discontent could indeed be a source of creative transformation.

17   M Seligman, *Authentic happiness: using the new positive psychology to realize your potential for lasting fulfillment*, Random House, Sydney, 2002, pp. 119–120.

18   L Boldt, *op. cit.*, pp. 18–26.

19 L Boldt, *op. cit.*, pp. 95–102. Boldt explores this idea further and suggests that we have a series of life scripts that are like organising principles that control the switchboard of your mind. Life scripts determine which data from the environment will be allowed into conscious awareness and which will be rejected. Boldt recommends setting definite life goals. These change your awareness by setting up new criteria to use for screening your calls or determining what will enter into conscious awareness.

20 N Branden, *Six pillars of self-esteem*, Bantam, New York, 1994. Branden claimed to have written the defining work on self-esteem and certainly does a good job of exploring the theoretical construct. However, later research by RW Tafarodi and WB Swann, Jr, ('Self-liking and self-competence as dimensions of global self-esteem: initial validation of a measure', *Journal of personality assessment*, no. 65, 1995, pp. 322–342) suggests that self-esteem is actually supported by two constructs: self-liking and self-competence.

21 TA Harris, *I'm ok — you're ok*, Random House, London, 1967.

22 D Sirota, LA Mischkind and MI Meltzer, *The enthusiastic employee: how companies profit by giving workers what they want*, Wharton Education, New Jersey, 2005.

23 G Hedlund in S Ghosahl and E Westney (eds), *Organization theory and the multinational corporation*, St Martin's Press, New York, 1993.

24 J Ridderstråile and K Nordström, *Funky business: talent makes capital dance*, Pearson Education, London, p. 167.

25 T Richardson, A Vidaurreta and T Gorman, *Business is a contact sport; using the 12 principles of relationship asset*

management to build buy-in, blast away barriers, and boost your business, Pearson Education, USA, 2002.

26 K Thomson, *op. cit.*, p. 120.

27 T Richardson, A Vidaurreta and T Gorman, *op. cit.*, p. 83.

28 CJ Butler and PS Chinowsky, 'Emotional intelligence and leadership behavior in construction executives', *Journal of Management in Engineering*, vol. 22, no. 3, September 2006, pp. 119–125.

29 D Goleman, R Boyatizis and A McKee, *The new leaders: transforming the art of leadership in the science of results*, Little Brown, London, 2002, p. 20.

30 KA Nair, 'Higher standard of leadership: lessons from the life of Gandhi', Berrett-Koehler, San Franscisco, 1994, pp. 80–1, as cited by RK Cooper and A Sawaf in *Executive EQ: emotional intelligence in business*, Texere, London, 1997, p. 63.

31 T Richardson, A Vidaurreta and T Gorman, *op. cit.*, p. 89.

32 As cited by RK Cooper and A Sawaf in *Executive EQ: emotional intelligence in business*, Texere, London, 1997, p. 52.

33 R Peterson, as quoted in T Peters, *The Tom Peters seminar*, Vintage, New York, 1994, pp. 240–1.

34 RK Cooper and A Sawaf, *op. cit.*, pp. 69–71.

Index

RocheMartin®
Building Emotional Capital

ECi™

The Emotional Capital Inventory (ECi™) represents an innovation in the measurement of emotional intelligence and leadership behaviors. The ECi™ and ECi 360™ are an exciting advance in our ability to measure the building blocks of emotional intelligence that are scientifically linked to the behaviors of successful leaders.

In only 10-12 minutes online, the ECi provides you with scores on the ten leadership competenceis found to be the skills that distinguish superior leaders from the rest.

EMOTIONAL CAPITAL REPORT

The Emotional Capital Report™ and Summary Report are leadership development tools that provide professional people with a comprehensive interpretation of their leadership potential based on their emotional intelligence. The reports include: a global Total Emotional Capital score; an individual's scores on ten emotional and social competencies linked to effective leadership, and a validity scale that measures positive response bias. The Emotional Capital Report also provides narrative descriptions of the leadership behaviors associated with each score; coaching strategies for developing emotional intelligence and leadership, and an action plan for designing a personal blueprint to build emotional capital.

RocheMartin®

ECi 360 MULTI-RATER REPORT

The 360 Multi-Rater Report combines responses from colleagues (Raters) and compares these scores to 'Self' scores to yield a gap analysis and an understanding of differences in self/other perception. The report also has a Verbatim Section containing open-ended questions that provide raters with the opportunity to elaborate on responses. Finally, a Coaching Section examines those particular factors where 'Self'' scores and Rater scores are significantly different and presents coaching strategies for improving leadership performance.

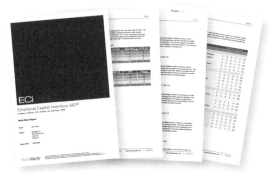

ECi SELECTION REPORT

The ECi Selection Report™ is an effective tool for talent identification and selecting high-performing employees. In addition to providing scores on the ten emotional and social competencies of emotional intelligence, the ECi Selection Report provides a guide to the interpretation of scores that can be explored during a behavioral interview. The interaction of high scores and low scores are explored in light of their potential impact on performance, and key follow-up questions are presented to guide the interview. A Summary Evaluation section provides an opportunity to evaluate the level of confidence in the candidate's emotional intelligence strengths and development needs as well as an opportunity for making recommendations.

For further information or to order directly online visit **www.rochemartin.com**   RocheMartin®

ECi & ECi 360 CERTIFICATION PROGRAM

The ECi & ECi 360 Certification Program is a 3-day program that provides comprehensive training in the administration and interpretation of the ECi and ECi 360. It introduces users to the concept of emotional capital and the relationship between emotional intelligence and leadership performance. The program covers the development of the inventory, psychometric properties, administration and interpretation procedures, including the application of the ECi and ECi 360 in the corporate context.

Workshops are held in Australia, Ireland, the United Kingdom, Europe, and United Arab Emirates.

For dates and locations of upcoming workshops visit **www.emotionalcapitalists.com**

EMOTIONAL CAPITALISTS – LEADERSHIP PROGRAM

An intensely practical 1-day workshop designed to accelerate the practice of emotionally intelligent leadership. The workshop examines the science of emotional intelligence (EQ) and the compelling business case for its relationship to leadership success. It is designed to equip participants with the ten dynamic emotional skills that distinguish outstanding leaders from the average.

The workshop remains sharply focused on the application and practice of the key strategies for building emotional intelligence and breaks open the building blocks of effective leadership skills.

To book a workshop for your organization go to **www.emotionalcapitalists.com**

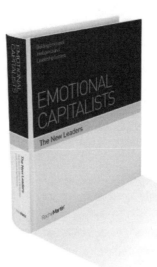

To learn more about these training tools or to attend a workshop, visit us at **www.emotionalcapitalists.com** or call **+61 3 9525 5252**

For further information or to order directly online visit **www.rochemartin.com**   **RocheMartin®**